BORN TO RISE

COMPILED BY

KIM FULLER

BORN
TO RISE

HOW 22 EXTRAORDINARY WOMEN
REWROTE THEIR STORIES, CLAIMED THEIR POWER,
AND FOLLOWED THEIR DREAMS

WORLDCHANGERS
M E D I A

Paperback: 978-1-955811-39-2
E-book: 978-1-955811-40-8
LCCN: 2023904865

First paperback edition: May 2023

Cover artwork: @NelliValova via AdobeStock and @daboost via AdobeStock
Cover design: Bryna Haynes
Layout and typesetting: Bryna Haynes
Editors: Monica Herald, Audra Figgins, Maggie Mills, Paul Baillie-Lane

Published by WorldChangers Media
PO Box 83, Foster, RI 02825
www.WorldChangers.Media

DEDICATION

This book is dedicated to every woman with a story to tell.
Your voice matters.

TABLE *of* CONTENTS

Rise into COURAGE

Rise into FREEDOM

Rise into CONNECTION

Rise into **GRACE**

INTRODUCTION

KIM FULLER

KEYDELL AND I STOOD side by side on the famous red circle carpet and took in the standing ovation from the TEDx audience. Wearing his best button-down shirt, he had one foot on his soccer ball and a huge smile on his face as he whispered in my ear, "This is awesome!"

"You deserve it," I murmured back. "Soak it in." I told myself the same thing.

Four months previously, I'd been standing in my photo studio with my client and friend Jeannie Spiro, preparing for her branding shoot for her website.

"How are you doing?" she asked.

I proclaimed, "I just finished my first book!"

It was hard for me to believe that those words had just come out of my mouth.

I never thought I would write a book. I was a photographer. Click, click, image made. Boom! Writing was tedious. It took too long.

And yet, about a year earlier, while working in the office I shared with my husband in the upper level of my studio, I'd heard a voice say, "*It's time.*"

I had never heard a voice like that before, but this was loud and clear. I gazed out into space and said aloud, "Are you kidding me?"

My husband Jim, startled, asked, "What? What's the matter?"

"The Universe wants me to write a book."

Jim laughed. So did I. But the next day, I sat down at my laptop and began to write.

The story which emerged was about our first two years with our son, Keydell. He joined our family of four when he was eight years old and our other two children were teenagers. I met him at a group home where a bunch of my female friends and I had been volunteering. He was so cute with his big brown eyes, tiny athletic frame, and feisty attitude. I loved him right away—even before I knew he would become my son.

At the same time, I was also working on becoming a bodhisattva, someone who aspires to reach enlightenment for the betterment of others. I dove into Buddhism after a brief encounter with the Dalai Lama while photographing one of his lectures. On his way to the stage, he paused where I was sitting and shook my hand. I felt as though pure love was holding me in that moment and became fascinated by how he could have that effect on me when he didn't even know me. As I listened to his talk, I connected immediately to the Buddhist teachings on compassion, impermanence, and how the path to relieve our suffering began with controlling our minds.

Wow! I wanted to know more. I wanted control of my mind. Who doesn't like control?

The next day, I began my meditation practice. Without any idea what I was doing, I sat and waited for a state of bliss to descend. Of course, that did not happen. I was uncomfortable, my thoughts were loud, and I had no idea if I was doing it right. I liked doing things right—to the point where my sisters labeled me "the perfect child" as a kid. The idea that I was doing meditation wrong made me highly uncomfortable. But I sat every day, and after a few weeks I noticed a shift, not only in myself but in my household. It seemed like my children and my husband were benefiting from my meditation practice, too. We were all more relaxed, less reactive, and happier.

From there, I was inspired to seek out a teacher. I figured I'd find a monk, a guru of some sort, who could give me direction. I read all the books, took a week-long course with the Dalai Lama, and found a group of friends who also followed the Buddhist teachings.

The more I practiced, the more I realized exactly how blessed I was. I came from a safe, loving family, was mentally stable, and had a thriving photography business. Life was good—but I knew that to really understand life, and to have the capacity to enlighten and uplift others, I had to understand suffering. I asked the Universe to show me some.

That's when I met Keydell.

The first two years of Keydell being in our home were the most challenging of my life. Prior to becoming part of our family, Keydell had suffered one traumatic experience after another. He'd had many different caregivers over the years; this resulted in very low self-esteem, no control over his life, and an intense fear of rejection. Yet, here he was in this whole new family who looked nothing like him and had no firsthand understanding of his world.

His behaviors reflected his trauma—and every ounce of my being was tested. I put my Buddhist practices of compassion, empathy and kindness into action. I failed often, and epically.

Everything I was practicing I was sharing with him. Together, we worked on noticing our stories and internal narratives. What kinds of thoughts and beliefs were driving our actions? Were our thoughts based in reality, or were they born from our habits and conditioning? What did we believe about ourselves that kept us in fear versus love? Could we be more compassionate and kinder to ourselves when we screwed up?

That last one was a biggie. I carried a ton of blame and shame about many of my behaviors.

After each behavioral episode, Keydell and I would both be exhausted. He was in such a heightened state of survival that it took all his energy to fight and feel some sense of control. I was starting to see I had little control except around what I thought about my experience. I too was afraid to let go of how things "should" be in our family and with this young son of mine. I yelled, often. I sometimes lost my shit completely. What kind of a Buddhist was I? In those moments where Keydell was in an outrage, it was so hard to stay present in the moment and not get caught up in my negative story of, "I screwed up again! My son is never going to find happiness."

It took a while—but I practiced letting go and just leaned into loving him, as he was, as I was. Jim and our other two amazing kids did the same. We all loved him, and slowly, he learned to love himself.

And then, the damned voice of the gods told me to write a book.

I knew it was what I needed to do, of course. I'd learned so much about Keydell's condition throughout our journey and wanted to help others keep their adopted children safely in their homes. It was the first time I'd ever told the whole story of our journey. Day by day, I revisited those challenging years. A year later, I had written a whole book.

Back to that day in my studio ...

Jeannie listened as I excitedly shared about the book, and we proceeded with her photo shoot. I thought nothing more about our conversation. Then, about a week later, I got an email from Jeannie asking if I wanted to apply to do a TEDx talk. She was on the search committee for the New Bedford, Massachusetts event, and immediately thought of me.

While I was flattered, I felt a wave of fear come over me. "Seriously? My first speaking gig could be a TEDx talk? What am I, nuts?" All this, and I hadn't even applied yet. But somehow, I knew it was going to happen. All I had to do was say yes—to the invitation, and to myself.

I applied, and was accepted.

I got out big, white sheets of paper, wrote down all my bullet points, and then immediately crossed them out. I paced around my living room for hours trying to figure out what my "angle" would be. What did I want the audience to feel, think about, and learn from my experience? This felt like a legacy kind of thing. Millions of people might see this talk on YouTube. I was already sweating and ripping my hair out, and I still had months to go.

I wanted to sound smart. I wanted to wow people. I wanted to be the coolest chick ever to grace that stage. But as I did the work to calm my wild ego and tuned into my heart, I began to connect the dots of all the experiences that had shaped the way I now lived.

I realized that my story was more than just what happened. It was how I practiced leaning into love, getting out of my own way and being present and trusting that I was not alone on my journey. I wanted to leave the audience with the message to love unconditionally, with compassion and empathy, because it was literally love that helped us find an acceptance and understanding of Keydell's pain, trauma, and behaviors, and ultimately healed our family.

After several weeks, I finally got my story out. I felt a huge shift within myself. I could see how my challenges had stretched me, helped me get to know and love myself, and shown me how strong and patient I was. My mindful meditation practice continued, and I was able to apply a deeper awareness and presence for my photography clients as well as with my family. Staying present and loving relieved me of my need to "fix" or take responsibility for things that were not mine. I could simply hold space for people without judgment or expectations and listen to them as they processed their stories and struggles.

When I finally walked out onto that TEDx stage and looked out into the dimly lit theater, I felt ready to share my story.

"Would you mind coming together for a deep breath?" I asked the audience.

We breathed together.

"Thank you. That was more for me than for you, but I appreciate you joining me."

I wasn't alone. They were listening, holding space for my story. I invited Keydell onto the stage just before my final line to show everyone how great he was doing. He dribbled his soccer ball out as the crowd stood and cheered. Our story had moved them, inspired them, and given them hope. Keydell didn't have to say a thing; he just stood in his story with confidence. We had come such a long way, and in that moment, I felt my story transform me from victim to hero and give Keydell a realization of how strong and brave he had been over the past few years. Our story inspired and educated the audience. Something surely to celebrate.

After my talk, nothing profound happened. The phone didn't start ringing off the hook with invitations to do more talks. The video did not go viral. However, I felt a sense of expansion and a release of control. I was proud of myself for saying yes to adopting our son, writing a book, and standing on a TEDx stage. I had stepped into my fears and turned towards love for myself—and, by doing so, I felt better able to love others. I did share the story several more times at my book signings. Each time I shared, I felt more healed and whole. More, I saw from audiences' responses that my story was having an impact.

The process of writing my fifteen-minute talk was even more powerful than writing the book. It was a process of pulling out the most important parts of my life and stringing them together to see how they formed me into who I am now. I have had a wild ride in life, moving often with my Navy family, living on a boat, photographing incredible people, and meeting the Dalai Lama and a child who was a great spiritual teacher. I felt a release of some of the pain of the past few years and saw my life as a whole—a whole lot of lessons, and joys, and love. I knew I could do the hard stuff, and that the Universe and all the people in my life had my back. Like so many things I have learned, I wanted to share this experience with others and thus Born to Rise was formed.

I started by gathering women to share personal stories in community, which built compassion, empathy, love, and support. No one needed to fix anyone else. They simply needed to love and listen.

I was doing more of this myself, and as I did, my life seemed to be in flow. My fears lessened, my worries about money, acceptance, being enough, began to fade. I had a purpose that was greater than myself.

I needed an inspiring name for this movement I was creating, so I asked the wildly magical Universe for a name and stayed present for the answer.

One night, while my husband and I were sitting in the theater waiting for the movie to start, a car ad came on the screen. The voiceover said, "This car is great, will take you on adventures, blah, blah, blah … because *you were born to rise!*"

That was it: the perfect name for my new venture. So what if it came from a car ad?

We are *all* born to rise. This is our purpose on Earth. When we are willing to look at the truth of who we are, love ourselves, and then share that love with others, we rise. When we live with courage versus fear, we rise. When we live with love and share our stories to educate, inspire, and connect with others in the ways we were meant to as human beings, we rise.

This, indeed, felt like the path of a bodhisattva.

***

The stories you are about to read are from women who have risen. They heard a calling from their souls and hearts that asked them to do something courageous—and, like I did, they listened. They trusted their callings. It wasn't always easy, and it didn't always happen all at once, but they knew that what was coming up for them was for their highest good. Now, they are sharing what is needed with the world in the ways only they can deliver it.

So many of us follow an expected path based on input from outside of ourselves. When this path is no longer in alignment with our soul, we can end up feeling empty, unhappy, and without purpose. This is where you get to rewrite the story you want to live.

Trigger warning: some of these stories visit the realms of mental health challenges (including suicidal ideation), childhood trauma, sexual assault, death and dying, divorce, and other sensitive topics. These descriptions are not intended to stir up drama or trauma for you as a reader, but to provide the background and context for each author's personal rise. If any of these topics may be triggering or challenging for you, I suggest that you read at places and times where you feel mentally and emotionally supported—or, better yet, alongside a trusted friend. Ultimately, each story in this book is a tale of hope and love, and we hope that you will experience them that way.

My intention is that these stories inspire you to listen to that inner voice that speaks when it's time to do something scary, challenging, or just plain unexpected, no matter what is currently transpiring in your life. May this book help you gain the courage to process, transform, and share your own story—because your story matters.

HERstory and the Rebirth of Feminine Voices

Until recently, history was written almost entirely by, and for, men.

The stories we know as "history" are male stories, from a male perspective. They center around war, conquest, politics, leadership, and the bold, fierce men whose deeds reverberate across the ages (for better or worse).

These are valuable stories. But they're not the *only* stories that can, and should, be told.

Women's stories are the stories of the heart—of love, transformation, community, and the exploration of inner realms. Our "HERstory" isn't so much about what we did, but how we felt. It's the story of what it means to come home to ourselves.

Women don't conquer; we gather.

My Born to Rise platform is designed to elevate women's voices, and this book is a part of that mission. As you'll soon see, the women who contributed their wisdom to this book are accomplished, brilliant, and mission-driven. Yet, you won't find stories of the external metrics of conquest and achievement in these pages; instead, you'll find profound, tender, and deeply moving recollections of the journey, and what it means to rise.

It is my intention that this book creates a sense of belonging for you. When you turn the last page, you will understand what it means to rise from the inside out and commit to a life rooted in authenticity, creativity, trust, and love. My hope is that you will carry the lessons from our authors' journeys with you into your own life, and know that you, too, are born to rise.

Rise into

COURAGE

IT'S MY BIRTHDAY.
WILL YOU TAKE MY PICTURE?

ALEXA GORMAN

"IT'S MY BIRTHDAY. Will you take my picture?"

I didn't plan to say it, to tell anyone, to call attention to the fact that I was alone, in a foreign country, where I spoke barely broken Spanish. A pathetic little girl with her overstuffed backpack, hiking boots, self-help audiobooks playing on repeat, and way too many crystals scraping against her back. A shell of her former self, putting all of her hope into this week to fix everything.

The sun was barely rising over the Andes when I reached Machu Picchu. I blinked back tears, feeling lonely, proud, sad, and victorious all at once.

Elvis, my Peruvian guide, wore a white cone-shaped hat made of alpaca wool that stretched at least eight inches over his head. He smiled at me with pity—a look I'd spent so much time running from, but couldn't escape.

I spread my arms to the camera, and grinned with my entire face, my entire body, my entire being. I felt my heart beginning to glow again as I embraced the full moment—my grief and anger, but also the pride I felt for getting here, for seeing a manifestation come to fruition. I knew I wasn't alone anymore. After years of isolation from my family, friends, my spirit, and my dreams, I understood that this wasn't the end of my healing journey, but the beginning.

A few months earlier, I squirmed between sitting and lying on the brown leather couch in my therapist's office, feeling like I couldn't spend another moment inside of my body. I hated her question, her insistence on getting an answer out of me. I hated that she pushed me to think about these things and held me accountable to the answers I gave. I knew it was helping, sure, but sessions had never been this uncomfortable until this point.

"What do you want?"

"No, not 'what do others expect of you.' What do you want?"

"Alexa, tell me what you want to do?"

I squirmed, and shrank, and curled myself into a ball. I almost knocked over my coffee mug on the side table. I watched the liquid slosh as I sat up and tried to steady it: a cup of coffee with one cream and one sugar. Sometimes, I like my coffee with a flavor shot and one cream, no sugar. Sometimes, I prefer a sugary caramel latte with whipped cream and sprinkles.

There was a time when I couldn't have told you how I took my coffee, only how he wanted me to have it, how he expected me to order it, and how disappointed he'd look if I strayed from those expectations. How I wrote in my journal in January before everything fell apart: *I'm afraid that I am not capable of living my own life and not feeling like he's my everything... I'm afraid that if left to my own devices, I'll fail, or never try to accomplish anything. I'm afraid that somehow, my willpower and drive are connected only to him, and not myself at all.*

I stared at the ceiling, wishing to be anywhere else in that moment, even if it meant being back in the comfort of a life that I lost myself in for 1,717 days, give or take a week or two.

I took a breath and threw up the answer I didn't realize I'd been smothering.

"I want to run my business. I want to stay in my house. I want to go to Machu Picchu on my birthday."

I drove home, still in a fog, but knowing I reclaimed something in that moment, a piece of me from before, who wanted to see the world—to relish in the wonders, the nature, the beauty, the pain, the grief, the love, the joy—all of it. I sat in my car after pulling into the driveway and Googled, "What country is Machu Picchu in?"

For the next three months, I managed to set fire to my income, the few friendships that remained after the separation, and anything that reminded me of him, or them, or what happened. It didn't stop the questions from family and friends, or their pitying looks. It didn't stop the bills we were supposed to share from bursting out of my mailbox, inbox, and voicemail box. It didn't stop the nightmares replaying the final moments, the words that played over and over again.

Me: *Please, can we try to fix this? I want to fix this. We can figure this out.*

Him: *I don't want to.*

I needed this trip to save me, to put me back together, to fill the holes, to mark the end of the healing journey. I needed it to be over; I needed this to be my grand entrance into the next chapter of my life.

I've ignored my intuition in the past. For years, I shut out the nudges and subtle signs (and the big, honking billboard-sized signs, too). I told myself that it wasn't realistic; that it didn't match what he was plotting and I was planning for our future together; that I didn't deserve things that good, or a life that wonderful.

And then, those nudges showed me the relationship was over, and that the man I'd married had actually been manipulating me away from my true self. I was so afraid to listen to my inner knowing, my intuition, my guides.

I crumpled on the kitchen's cold tile floor as the truth finally hit me head-on: I couldn't hide in his manipulations or my delusions anymore. I was alone in my head for the first time in years, left to create something out of this unknown reality.

As I unpacked the memories, the moments that led up to the end, I felt like I was flaying myself open, one appendage at a time. I was desperate to understand how I got here; how someone who joked about wanting to be single forever, to travel alone, who respected her independence above all else, turned into this shell of a bitch who couldn't crawl from one side of her 900-square-foot house to her bed because her chest was too heavy and her breath came too short. How she couldn't sleep unless her two dogs laid on either side, pinning her legs in place. How the owners of the liquor store told her they missed her if she hadn't been in to pick up a jug of Carlo Rossi White Zinfandel every few days. How she woke from nightmares that were only flashbacks of her true self chipping away.

I didn't know why, but I knew I had to jump feet-first and trust that, even if the landing wasn't graceful, I would land safely. It was the only way to rebuild trust in myself, my intuition, my independence, and my rebirth after burning it all to the ground.

So, I went. I shoved clothes, crystals, my journal, oracle card decks, and the various emergency safety supplies my mom and I bought during a frantic Walmart trip into a backpack. I was clumsy, and every time I hauled the backpack from the floor or the overhead compartment onto my back—while simultaneously apologizing and hoping I didn't whack people too hard while unaware of how wide I was—I regretted the thirty-plus pounds of stuff I'd brought.

I felt excited and anxious, like a child in the early hours of Christmas morning: not knowing what to expect, but feeling the love and magic only felt on truly special days.

I toured Cusco city alongside a group of women celebrating their fiftieth birthdays. They called me brave, and whispered with wide eyes when they thought I was out of earshot.

I climbed Vinicunca, known as Rainbow Mountain, and cried at the top, because it was the hardest hike I'd ever climbed and I was damn proud of me, yet I felt the judgment from the locals offering pony rides all the way to the summit. When we reached the almost-peak and our tour guide stopped, saying we were free to climb the rest of the way or take a rest until we began the journey down, I plopped my backpack down and half-crawled my way to the peak.

On the way down, I talked with a woman who'd just divorced her husband of more than thirty years because she wanted to travel and "live the rest of her life instead of sitting in a recliner," so she did. She and her daughter bought me dinner and shared tips for solo travel. They made me feel less alone, and less crazy, and validated not only my choice to reclaim myself but my choice to do this leg of the journey alone.

To get to Machu Picchu from Cusco, you have to wake up at like 3:00 a.m., take a cab to a train, then hop on a bus that brings you to the entrance of the site. When I disembarked from the train, I was greeted by a huge yellow rose bush—a sign from my late father, who passed away in 2011. He called me Alexa Rose and always gifted me a dozen yellow roses for birthdays, special occasions, and celebrations.

When I met Elvis at the bus stop, his sign said Alexa Rose instead of my last name.

After he led me and two Bulgarian tourists through the site, we stopped to take more photos, and I pulled out my oracle cards. Staring at the Wounded Healer card, I cried as I read the description, "You are a healer; your situation is being resolved; the roots grow deepest where the wind blows strongest."

Sometimes, I receive soft, gentle, reassuring signs like yellow roses. Sometimes, billboards like the Wounded Healer card hit me in the face.

At the beginning of the week, I ordered takeout food at every restaurant, not wanting to be seen eating alone. On my last night, I sat down at a small cafe, clumsily ordered soup and tea, and ate by myself with steady hands, comfortable in the quiet while I scratched notes in my journal.

When I packed my bag the night before my flight, it seemed lighter somehow. Maybe I was just stronger.

Sitting in a cafe at the airport in Lima the next morning, I read the bulleted notes on my phone and began to reconstruct the week. It felt like I had no choice but to move forward, climb up, look ahead. I missed the Andes already; I mourned the trip's end.

I didn't feel ready to leave ... and due to a bank error and missed deposit, I almost didn't. Thankfully, I was no longer ashamed to call on my support system to help me make the last legs of the journey, and the issue was resolved with something approaching grace.

My experience in Peru was not the end of my healing journey, as I intended. It wasn't the storybook ending; I didn't come home and instantly create a successful business, buy a house, and skip into the sunset with a new, healthy partner.

But a few weeks after returning, I walked into a bar to meet an old friend. I took a deep breath, ordered a glass of wine and told him the whole story, from start to finish. I shared truths I'd kept in the dark for years, no longer feeling ashamed of what I lived through, or how I survived. I didn't hold back to save myself from embarrassment. I wasn't afraid of looks of pity.

My wounds weren't healed, but they were better. I was a lot closer to understanding who I was and how I wanted to live, but I was still three career changes from becoming a full-time business owner. And all of that was okay, because I walked into that bar and sat down, unafraid of telling my truth in its entirety, knowing that I had everything I needed to put the rest of the pieces back together in my own time.

Peru wasn't the end that I'd hoped for, but the start of a long journey back home to myself. Each step I took up the Andes prepared me for the daily decisions I would make upon returning, as I learned to release the fears of how I'd be perceived, and to trust that

I am capable of putting one foot in front of the other and creating my path from here.

A healing journey, as I've come to understand, doesn't have a finish line. My trust in myself ebbs and flows. Some days, I feel like that part of my story didn't actually happen to me. Other days, I wake up needing time to reorient to my current reality. The most difficult part will always be having patience with myself, and trusting that things can, will, and are working out. I bring myself back home to the moment by focusing not on what's no longer true, but what is true today: I am safe. I am loved. I am free. I create my own reality.

Day by day, my confidence grows. My faith in myself grows. Never in a linear fashion. Never without trial and error. And that's the journey.

Regardless of how difficult things get, I am not incapable, or broken, or unable to recover. This journey may not come to a fairy-tale end, but the healing journey ahead will open up so much more than an ending ever could.

I DON'T WANT TO BE MARRIED ANYMORE

PARCHELLE TASHI

IT WAS A WARM OCTOBER NIGHT in San Diego, one of those nights when rolling down the window in the car and letting the California breeze cool us down was a no-brainer. I remember thinking to myself in gratitude, *I'll never get tired of this. It feels like home.*

My husband Cliff and I had finished unpacking the rest of our moving boxes and successfully loaded everything else into a U-Haul storage unit. It was official. We were San Diegans, and I couldn't wait to get back to our newly leased, first floor apartment in Carmel Valley to crash for the night. It was starting to feel like the new beginning we both needed.

He drove our burgundy Ford Expedition slowly out of the huge storage unit parking lot, as I typed our new address into Google

Maps. I set my phone on the dashboard so he could see and leaned back in the passenger seat. Thankfully, we were just ten minutes away from home.

Being closer to Cliff's amazing son Cjae, who was ten at the time, was the main motivation for the move. Since he was five, he'd spent summers with us in Chesapeake, Virginia, and in Philadelphia. The place we found in San Diego was close enough for him to ride his bike from school to see us whenever he wanted, instead of dealing with a long plane ride.

With a foreclosure, late payments, and two repossessions on my report, and child support arrears and repossessions on his, it was a miracle we even got approved for an apartment in Carmel Valley. It was one of the most expensive areas to live in the city, almost three times the rent and a third the size of our three-story row home in Philly.

As we drove away from the storage unit, I began thinking about what I needed to make deep-fried Oreos, one of Cjae's favorites that I'd always make especially for him. Cliff was in one of his moods again, though. As we were leaving the storage unit, we got into a disagreement over the boxes, and then he said it.

"I'm at a crossroads," he said as we pulled up to a stop sign.

I looked at the GPS and said, "It says to make a right."

"No, I'm at a crossroads in our relationship."

My head shifted back while my eyes scrunched and squinted at the same time. It felt like a for-real record scratch moment followed by me saying, "Okay ... What do you mean?"

We were still sitting at the stop sign. He blurted out the response like he'd been holding it in for a long time, "I don't want to be married anymore."

I stared ahead into the intersection while he made the right turn. The rest of the car ride was mostly silent. I didn't say much else; I didn't know what to say. I was just so confused. I did, however, finally understand what a "deer in headlights" moment was, because I for sure didn't see this coming.

I must not be hearing this right, I thought to myself. We'd just moved into this new apartment. I had busted my ass to get the money together for the deposit and was the one responsible for finding the storage unit I could see in the side view mirror behind us. Maybe he was having some kind of breakdown.

That moment was the first shock that would send my world as I had known it (and built it) crashing down.

On the outside, I had been a good Christian wife throughout our seven years of marriage. On the inside, to be married was totally about what people thought about us—about me. For years I wore the wife badge proudly and often remarked to people, "Oh, my husband this-and-that," or, "I'll ask my husband about it." It was a status thing, especially in the church, and I put most of my value on how my marriage looked to other people.

In truth, I paid a pretty penny to maintain that image.

I was with an attractive black man who was a single father, went to church, loved God, could make me laugh, and had great legs. As far as I was concerned, I was winning. Our marriage was challenging most of the time, but I truly believed we could figure it out and be happy. He was "voluntarily unemployed" for some time, almost refusing to find work because it would not allow him to make music. Communication was also tough, and I was in the dark most of the time about what he was thinking. When he'd get in his moods, he

23

wouldn't say what was going on and would give me the cold shoulder with no explanation. When it came to sex … well, that was also awkward, because I felt like I couldn't be a sexy, feminine chick, although I tried for him.

On the list of what I thought I needed to do to be a good wife was having a child. My husband talked about how he wanted to have a girl, and even kept a dress he'd bought for her before we met. I figured having a child would make him happier and motivate him in some way, so I went through many unsuccessful fertility treatments and tests. This wasn't cheap either, and felt even more burdensome considering I paid just about every household bill on my teacher's salary in Virginia, and later as a producer for my mentor's business in Philly. After I lost that job, we quickly fell three months behind on rent.

If I tried to talk to him about contributing to the household bills, or ask about his job search, he might stop speaking to me for weeks or even a month. So, I only brought up those questions on occasion, put my head down, and took care of everything else on my own.

All of this was unfolding behind the picture of a young, talented, and beautiful Black Christian couple who served faithfully in church.

But there were still more secrets: for me, being married was more than just about my status as a wife; I felt like it stood as a barrier between me and the questions anyone (including myself) would have about my sexuality.

***

It was raining outside one day in kindergarten during recess, so the teachers let us play indoors before nap time. Kids were all spread about, some playing with toys, others running around, some playing jump rope. I was on the bleachers next to my classmate, another little brown girl, Koren, who really liked to play make-believe games.

"Let's pretend to drive a car. I'll be the mommy and you be the daddy! Okay, you gotta be on this side so you can drive. But you have to open the door for me first," Koren instructed me. Innocently, I played along; at five years old, this experience undoubtedly and innocently left an imprint on me.

Growing up, I was the geek-jock-tomboy who admired seeing women like Queen Latifa, MC Lyte, and Aaliyah, who didn't wear flowery dresses and heels; I loved their style and how they carried themselves. Feminine *and* masculine.

My parents dubbed out any profanity or nudity from the movies they recorded onto VHS, so I had very little knowledge about sex, let alone what it meant for two women to be together in a romantic relationship. What I remember resonating with me most was how men swooned over Khadijah James in *Living Single*. In a way, it gave me hope that I could express myself as a masculine woman and be in a relationship with a man too. That's exactly what I created with Cliff.

The night before our wedding in December 2010, I dreamt of waking up to a beautiful, soft-skinned dark woman in a large bedroom with floor-to-ceiling windows that overlooked a view of lush greenery. I couldn't fully see her face, but she looked over at me, smiled, got out of the bed, and walked across the room to the bathroom.

I had no idea where I was or what any of it meant, but I remember how at home and in love I felt. It was all so real in the dream that I felt like I'd been cheating on my soon-to-be husband. I had never met this woman I saw in the dream and there was no one I could tell about it, especially on the day of my wedding. I wrote it off as a result of that spicy chicken ball from the bachelorette party, and went on to marry Cliff on a snowy day in Virginia Beach.

***

In the weeks after Cliff's shocking announcement, I held on to the idea that this was just a phase he was going through. He was sitting at the dining table one night immersed in his phone, and I walked up to the side of the table and asked in a soft, open tone, "Hey, are you sure you want to do this?"

A few seconds of silence filled the room, and suddenly it got a little chilly. Before he could answer, I continued, "Because it's not making sense why you would do this when we just moved here. Maybe someone can help you decide if this is what you want to do. Can we just sit down with someone?"

"Who, like a therapist?" he asked with an annoyed tone.

I didn't want to go back and forth on this, and with desperation in my voice replied, "Yes. Please."

Surprisingly, he agreed, and the next week I found an older Black male therapist who helped couples. I really wanted to give this my best shot, considering I didn't have the money or insurance to do an extended number of sessions, and didn't want to hear from Cliff that he couldn't relate to the person helping us. I wanted to eliminate all of that and give us the best opportunity to figure this out.

"Let's say this room represents your relationship," said Dr. Brown. He had long salt-and-pepper locs and professor-y glasses, and sat with his leg crossed, clipboard resting on his right knee. The room was colorful, with interesting art pieces and a small water fountain trickling in the background.

He uncrossed his legs, leaned towards Cliff, and continued, "If the corner represents you wanting to be in this marriage, and outside the door represents you being out of it, where would you say you are?"

We were seated on a blue IKEA loveseat, perfectly sized for two people to be either close or apart but still on the same couch. My heart sank back into my chest, and I could feel it beating heavier and heavier. Before I could calm down and brace myself for his answer, he said, "I'm at the door."

I turned to him in disbelief—not only at the fact that he'd said it, but at how *quickly* he'd said it. That hurt more than the announcement itself.

It was then that I woke up to my own reality: I'd followed the rules, got screwed, and lost myself in the process. We were sitting with this therapist because I'd asked him, "Are you sure about this?" But I'd never asked *myself* that question, or really thought about what I wanted next.

There were two people in my life who truly knew what was going on. One of them was Jenna, my very first friend in San Diego and my best friend to this day.

"Ah, *hell* no!" she said, when I spilled the tea to her one night after we'd finished playing basketball at the YMCA. "Do you need me to come get your stuff? What's the plan?"

I didn't know what I wanted, but my girl Jenna helped me see that I had permission to do what I needed to do for myself, which was empowering and scary at the same time.

What made sense to me was to tell Cliff to take the second bedroom, pay his half of the rent, and get his cell phone bill in his name. It became clear to me that it was okay to focus on myself and what I wanted. This was a new concept for me considering my church conditioning taught me to place God first, others second, and myself third.

For some people, church and religion is a saving grace and foundation for community. For some, it's about a closer relationship with God. For me, it was a way of life I became accustomed to at a young age, and eventually became the force behind the very high standards I placed on myself in order to be accepted and fit in.

From age seventeen, all the way up to age thirty, I became quite good at fitting in. In those years of my life, I was not a Christian who went to church on Sunday after partying at the club and having sex with strangers on Saturday. I was the one who was early to service and the last one to leave. I never left the house without my Bible, didn't touch drugs or alcohol, erased all my secular music from my devices, didn't copy CDs (because that was stealing), sang in the choir, and hardly missed a service or a Bible study night. My mom expected me to attend her church, but during my senior year of high school, I would get up at 7:00 a.m. on Sundays, sneak out of the house to attend the church I preferred, then meet my family at their church for the 11:00 a.m. service.

During the biggest party nights at Virginia Tech, where I went to school, I wasn't at the parties. Instead, I was outside the parties offering to pray with people, inviting them to church or to accept Jesus as their Savior. I led Bible studies, had disciples assigned to me, was president of the campus choir, and advised other young women to avoid holding hands or kissing anyone because it would lead to fornication.

Even my mom said, "It don't take all that!"

To me, it did.

Little did I know that my religion would become such a deep-rooted part of my life and identity, not only as a confused young girl who searched for understanding and hated wearing dresses, but as a fully-grown woman. All throughout college and while married, I went to church more than my family ever did.

Once Cliff and I separated, I began to see the real reason we were together in the first place: we were meant to free each other from the grip of religion, which had trapped us both in a life we didn't want. Even though I was too deep in to see it at the time, Cliff had the courage to speak up, and for that I'm forever grateful to him. Cliff grew up in a church where the pastor could beat the kids; even though he was talented, he wasn't allowed to play drums or piano because he didn't speak in tongues. After our separation, I saw him embrace his freedom in big steps, doing things that were previously taboo—like getting his ears pierced, getting a couple tattoos, and stepping up in his music.

When I was studying at Virginia Tech, I would often tell myself that it was a good thing I was there instead of at Georgia Tech, the school that rejected me—the school I really wanted to go to. To make myself feel better, I'd say, "Had I gone to Atlanta, I would've been wild and free. I probably would have been in a relationship with a woman with tattoos and short hair!"

Well, today, I wake up with the woman of my dreams, and I feel more at home and in love than ever before. And the wild, inquisitive girl inside me—the girl who hated wearing dresses and always wanted to take charge? Well, not only was she born to rise: she has arisen.

3

THROUGH LIFE'S STORMS

MICHELLE LEMOI

IT WAS CHRISTMAS MORNING, 2020.

Rain fell, varying from a soft and tender mist to a hard hammering, and I lay there feeling restless. Even after a difficult year, it was a feeling that had been with me for some time: a constant nagging deep in the pit of my stomach that I wasn't where I was meant to be, doing what I was meant to be doing. I wasn't who I was meant to be.

Thunk, thunk, thunk.

What was that sound? From my bedroom upstairs, I could tell it was coming from the main floor of the house.

Thunk, thunk, thunk.

Was it water dripping? Maybe. But not in the sink. No, this sound traveled some distance before it made contact.

What now? I thought as I dragged myself out of bed to investigate. *Thunk, thunk, thunk.*

Much to my dismay, I walked into my living room to find it was raining. Indoors. There was water everywhere, coming out of the white wood ceiling and onto my beautiful cherry hardwood floors. There were numerous leaks along a three-foot span.

My brain fought to process that this was the cause of the *thunk-ing.* My anxiety was high, my heart racing. I looked outside into the dark morning where sheets of rain continued to fall.

"*Of course* it's raining in my living room on Christmas morning," I shouted, exasperated.

I snapped into survival mode, picking up the mess, soaking up the water and strategically placing buckets and a painting drop cloth. I sighed heavily. This was all so familiar, and all so tiring. When was I going to catch a break? When was my life going to even out and not be drenched in woes and survival and struggle?

A few days later, a contractor came out to take an initial look at the damage. He called me, saying, "You aren't going to believe this!"

"Um, sure I will," I remarked, sitting in my car, waiting for the other shoe to drop.

"Looks like at some point, a tree branch fell and did some damage. But the previous guys left the branch inside the roof between the cathedral ceiling and the shingles. I've never seen anything like it!"

"Hmm," was all I could muster, accompanied by an eye roll. *Sounds expensive.*

He continued, "We can fix it no problem. It'll be $500."

"Done." My mood immediately lightened. I could breathe a sigh of relief and move forward. There was plenty else on my plate to worry about.

New Year's ushered in a hopeful 2021 and I carried on. But that restless feeling was still there. Things at work were rocky. I had found out in November—after laying off a third of my staff—that I was next on the list to go. For some time, I'd been feeling like all I was doing was grinding away at work, but I had announced to the Universe a few years back that I would stay at this job until 2024, when my son graduated high school. Then, I would be on to better things for myself. I needed the stability and income to rebuild my financial foundation after the devastating loss of my namesake business, Lemoi Erectors, in 2016.

I look back now and think the Universe must have laughed when I made that declaration. Clearly, that restless feeling was a marker for huge change looming in my near future.

Amid anxiety-inducing managerial reviews, there was more rain.

Thunk, thunk, thunk. I was asleep in the middle of the night when I heard it. I turned into the pillow, tears springing from my eyes, and listened once more to be sure my ears had not betrayed me. *Thunk, thunk, thunk.*

Dammit.

I leapt from bed and ran downstairs to see water everywhere again. Same routine. Same hustle to clean it up. Same anxious feelings. *Why does this keep happening?* Too tired to think any more about it, I decided to reach out to the contractor in the morning.

After the contractor's assessment, I came home to find a bright blue tarp tacked to my roof. There it would stay until the spring, when a larger area could be patched—or so I was told.

Several storms later, despite the tarp, water found its way in again. *Thunk, thunk, thunk.* Each time, my anxiety would shoot through the roof, and I would stress and get so upset, even though it was something I had very little control over.

As if to echo the literal rainstorms threatening my roof, there were thick clouds brewing at work too. By June, I had resigned. I felt untethered, angry, and anxious. My plan for the next several years was gone. My roof was still leaking. I had to take a job for significantly less pay to make ends meet. Then, the contractor informed me that the whole front of my roof would need to be replaced. There were more issues than previously discovered, to the tune of $6,600—a sum I absolutely did not have. Could half the roof be patched? No, it wasn't an option. Then, he stopped returning my calls.

I was so angry. I was only in year eleven of a thirty-year shingle roof. Why was all this happening? I felt adrift. Lost. Scared.

I decided to ignore the problem for the time being. Maybe I should sell the house and let it be someone else's problem? Maybe I should find a way to come up with the money to fix it? But, if the front part of the roof was bad, did that mean the rest of it would begin showing signs of needing repair?

Months went by, summer fading into fall, and my restlessness only increased. I did not feel I was in alignment with any kind of purpose. I felt trapped and stuck.

Winter was approaching. Each time it rained, my anxiety was high. The roof didn't always leak. But the staining on the ceiling, the tarp slowly shredding on the roof ... they reminded me that the roof wasn't protecting me or my son. I was living somewhere unstable, and it was continually getting worse.

Throughout winter and into spring, I kept myself in high gear, creating a new business to elevate women in the construction industry along with the new full-time job. Yet, the restlessness remained. Even worse, debt was starting to pile up both from the business creation and expenses and the cut in salary. I was feeling desperate. No matter how hard I tried to make things happen and push, push, push, my efforts went unrewarded. Despair crept into the center of my chest and wrapped itself around my gut. The sense of being adrift deepened. The weariness in my bones was like lead, heavy and burdensome.

I was so very tired. I was questioning everything.

Time kept moving though, and I found a new job that offered better financial security. Plus, not one event of dripping had occurred since the fall. *It must have fixed itself,* I reasoned. After thirty years in the construction industry, I knew full well there was no way that could be true. But ignoring the problem was kind of working, right? I lulled myself into thinking all would be okay—but then, while standing in my yard, looking at the tatters of the tarp blowing listlessly around the roof, I had a full-blown panic attack. I felt extremely unsafe and ungrounded. I ran into the house, grabbed my favorite blanket, and curled up on the couch.

What is this? It had been years since I'd experienced a panic attack. I explained it away, telling myself there was still that sense of restlessness inside. That the new job wasn't quite panning out the way I had anticipated, and left me with a lot of free time. That my business was in its early stages, so there was a lot of trying things and a waiting for results. Things would turn around. But my weariness was starting to manifest as insomnia, which kept my anxiety high and panic attacks rolling in on a regular basis. I knew the tightness in my chest, the upset stomach, and the weariness were my body yelling at me to pay attention. Something had to change.

I decided to take the summer off from my business. Little did I realize that taking time off would be the catalyst for significant and deep transformation within. I would uncover things I did not want to face and had done my very best to avoid at all costs.

The summer was unbearable. There were days I had multiple panic attacks, one after the other. I was fortunate that work was so slow because I was barely functioning some days. I would get done what I needed to, but when my list was checked off, I spiraled.

In those moments of intense fear, I realized I was suffering alone. My son didn't know what was going on. Friends were left in the dark. The only individual who had any inkling was my mental health counselor. I was ashamed, afraid, and alone. At the back of my mind was the constant reminder of the roof. While the summer was dry, the fact that I couldn't get it fixed nagged me and I felt helpless.

If I could only fix this one thing, maybe I will feel better, I told myself. *Maybe everything else will start to align if I can get rid of my constant worries about the roof.*

I reached out to the insurance company, and they wouldn't cover the external damages. They would fix the interior, but ... "Isn't that just patching over the problem?" I asked. "And what happens the next time it rains, and the water keeps coming in?" Another dead end.

I then spoke with a different roofing contractor, one that I knew had a solid reputation. He came out and assured me I needed new everything, and that it would cost $22,000. The silver lining? They offered financing. I smiled, breathing a sigh of relief ... until I was declined because I was still rebuilding my credit after the loss of my business.

My mental health counselor asked, "Do you see a pattern here?"

I sat in front of our Zoom call, bewildered, and shook my head.

She said, "I know how you are, my dear girl. You want every-thing fixed *right now.* You want all the answers. You want a plan. You want relief."

I nodded.

I was so worn down by the anxiety, the lack of sleeping and appetite, the panic, and the emotions that were swamping me. For the first time in my life—despite two divorces, losing my business, being a single mother, and surviving eighteen years of childhood trauma—I didn't know what the next steps were. *How can this be? Is this it? I've gone through all these things in life, but what if I can't go any further? Is this how people die, despair and hopelessness taking over until there's nothing left?*

My counselor continued, "You cannot do this alone. You need a small army of people you trust to help you through this transfor-mation. It's not going to be fixed overnight. You have to trust, to surrender, to deal with all those emotions stuck in your heart. You have been frozen for so long, defined by your work and your ability to do and make things happen. You are being called to free yourself of that, find your inner peace, and heal."

I sat there in shock, unable to breathe or move. She had thrown me a lifeline, and although it took a few moments, I grabbed hold—and for the next four months, I didn't let go.

My transformation journey broke me down to my very core. Everything I had ever believed about myself was upended and ques-tioned. I built my small army of caregivers and bared my soul. I dug in and went to work on my childhood trauma, learned breathwork, meditated, started taking holistic supplements for anxiety, and saw my mental health counselor sometimes three times a week.

I said goodbye to the new job and went back to the company I knew was a safe haven for me. I kept my business on hold for when my journey of healing would deliver me to solid ground.

All this work culminated in the realization that I needed a foundation for *myself*. I had built a house of cards that was based on external factors, like my work, with a blatant disregard for who I am. Like my roof, I had many patches added here and there. Sure, I had a self-care routine; sure, I had friends; and sure, I was successful, but none of it went to the core of who I was. It was superficial and unsustainable. Whenever a strong storm came, my foundation was too shaky to support me. Just like the roof, I would no longer be able to repair only the visible damage.

If I want to fix the roof, it needs the $22,000 overhaul. If I want to fix myself, I need to invest in my own well-being from the inside out, every single day.

I no longer get upset about the roof. (That's right: at the time of this writing, it's still in need of repair.) But no amount of worrying or overthinking is going to change that. I trust and know, when the timing is right, it will get replaced. I don't know when that will be, how it will be paid for, or any other specifics, but it *will* get fixed. I know that in my gut. Even as we approach another wet season, I know it's going to be okay.

As for me, I am still in the midst of my transformation and healing. Like my leaky roof, I still have broken parts. But I know now that I don't have to have all the answers. I only have to love and accept all of me.

Each and every day, through all of life's storms, I work at sustaining my inner peace and shoring up my foundation; this work will allow me to take bigger steps in the future. Only then will I find the pathway to being whole, and finally make peace with the restlessness.

4

CARDINALS

JEANNIE SPIRO

"HOW ARE YOU?" he asked gently.

Tears streamed down my cheeks. Before I could find words to reply, he asked again. "Jeannie. Are you okay?"

Where should I even begin? I wondered. *I'm ashamed. I'm absolutely petrified. I'm failing miserably. How do I even wrap words around how much I'm struggling right now?*

"No, Uncle John," I finally managed. "I'm not okay."

Six months earlier, on a beautiful April afternoon, I had marched into my boss's office and quit my part-time job. That job was supposed to be the bridge that allowed me the bandwidth and financial security to grow my coaching business and support my family before I leaped full-time into entrepreneurship.

I'd had a successful multi-decade career. Received a prestigious award mere months into my first sales position. Managed an all-women sales team without any prior leadership experience. Mastered the art of negotiation and saved clients millions of dollars. Patiently nurtured leads for years and closed them when the timing was right. Retained thousands of clients and made sure all were supported well. With all that under my belt, entrepreneurship should have been a walk in the park, right?

Obviously not.

I was forty-four when I felt the call to leave my corporate career. I wanted more from my life and my work, and was eager to find out how I might help other women like me spread their wings beyond the boardroom.

My timing was … less than ideal. With two children in private school, and college tuition looming, this wasn't the time to "follow my passion." But the more I ignored it, the louder the call became—until, one day, I found a coaching certification program that would set me on a straight path to helping the women I wanted to serve. I enrolled right then and there.

One certification followed another. While still working full-time, I quietly launched my business, website, and mailing list, and started attracting clients online.

It felt foreign at first, but also unbelievably exciting as my passion turned into a mission that made me come alive. I knew I was on the right path; while I was not quite settled in my niche, the strong foundation of sales and business skills I'd gained in my career made it so much easier to enroll and serve clients.

For three years, I was a full-time employee and part-time business owner, in addition to meeting my family's needs. It was a lot to manage, but I had the energy and passion for it all. I told myself that, one day, when I was making enough money in my business, I'd close the chapter on my career and leave it behind for good.

But that day never seemed to come. I constantly wrestled with the idea of quitting, but couldn't bring myself to pull the trigger. The money and security were too important.

Living a double life was hard. I spent my days negotiating insurance renewals and trying to save money for my corporate clients. I worried that my male competitors would discover my side hustle and swoop in to pluck my clients away. At the same time, every lunch break, evening, and weekend was devoted to supporting my coaching clients. I also enrolled in dozens of trainings, read hundreds of books, and traveled for conferences to learn everything I could about this new world of online business. After all, how could I teach my clients to do it unless I accomplished it first?

I was fulfilled by my growing business and craved more time with it. I was certain that this was where I was meant to be. But I wasn't even close to making enough to replace my salary. And so, I kept on going, burning both ends of the candle, waiting for something to shift so I could make a move.

In October of 2013, in my third year of juggling both business and job, my boss walked into my office and closed the door behind him.

"Jeannie," he began. "I've got some news."

He proceeded to tell me that he was closing my division and had sold it to someone we both knew. They'd made arrangements that included me going to work for this new company. While the new situation appeared to be ideal, I couldn't help but feel upset. I had been gearing up to quit on my own terms; this had thrown a wrench in the works.

When I got home that night, I shared the news with my husband. We both knew my business wasn't ready to support my portion of the family expenses, so there was only one thing to do: accept the new job.

Within weeks, I found myself completely overwhelmed as I juggled my old job, the new job, the transition, and all my coaching clients. It was brutal, stressful, and exhausting. I hated the new commute. Nor did I love working for the new company. All I wanted was to focus on my business and be with my daughter before she left for college in a few months.

As the New Year approached, my misery and stress turned to anger at myself that I hadn't done more to grow my business. This new job wasn't right for me, and I'd known it from the moment it was offered to me, but my fear had prevented me from listening to my gut. It was death by a thousand papercuts.

I needed to end the pain and take back my life.

In April of 2014, I crafted an exit plan that included designing, selling, and filling a coaching program that would replace my salary and provide the financial stability I needed to make this big leap. My business had suffered over the last few months, and my mental health was in poor shape. I had planned to wait a few months to make a move—but then, after one particularly horrible day at work, I marched into my boss's office and resigned in spectacular fashion. In that moment, I chose myself—and my business, too.

I'd like to say that this was the beginning of my happily-ever-after, but that was not the case. I struggled to fill that coaching program and had very few clients in the months that followed. I was on shaky ground and, while it was nice not to have to go to a job I hated every day, the financial stress was ratcheting up in a big way.

I spent that summer mourning what was coming: both children moving away to college, my husband gone at work all day, and me all alone in our house with only my failing business, our rising debt, and the threat of upcoming tuition payments and insurance premiums to keep me company. I kept pushing to enroll clients, but it was an uphill struggle.

Once the kids left for college, I discovered that I would indeed have company in my home office. My two coworkers, Lonely and Afraid, talked at me incessantly.

How did you get here? You were at the top of your game, and now you can barely hold on. You're selfish. You're stupid. You did this to yourself and your family. Karma's a bitch, and now you're paying the price.

Who do you think you are?

I felt as though I was traversing the bottom of the ocean without a mask, fins, or an air tank. I couldn't see my next steps. I couldn't see light at the surface. I was flailing, ashamed, and embarrassed that my Grand Plan had led me here. I'd felt so certain that I was making the right decision—and yet, here I was.

I'd cozied up with failure many times in the past, but this failure felt different than anything I'd experienced before. Those failures hadn't negatively affected my family. Nor had they been tied to what I still believed was my life's purpose. With each day that passed, I watched my dream of entrepreneurship slip away. If something didn't change soon, I would be forced to go back to corporate just to make ends meet.

I have a vivid memory of digging in my couch for spare change because I didn't have enough money to pay the bills. I'd gone from a multi-six-figure salary with massive benefits to … this.

And so, when I ended up on the phone with Uncle John that day, I wasn't just "not okay." I was barely hanging on.

His simple question opened the floodgates to my despair. I could no longer hold back the shame, fear, and exhaustion I'd been carrying.

"I'm failing miserably in my business," I gushed. "I'm not making enough money. I quit my job in a huff, thinking 'I can do this,' but I can't. I can't figure it out on my own. I can't find my way. I no longer have faith in myself—and the worst part is that I'm sitting between this passion I have and the purpose I thought I was meant to pursue, and I'm failing the people I love most. I'm *failing them*, and everywhere I look, all I see is my failure staring back at me."

I paused for a breath to stem the torrent. Then, I asked, "What do you do when you no longer have faith, Uncle John?"

It was a hard question to ask. Because, you see, Uncle John was an ordained Catholic priest. Faith was his specialty.

He was silent for a moment. Then, he told me, "I'll send a check to cover your health insurance for this month and next. There's more if you need it, too. You only have to ask."

I was overwhelmed by his generosity, and said so.

But he wasn't done. He began coaching me on how to reignite my faith in myself, and also in something bigger than myself. "Imagine that the water you see flowing from your faucet is money coming into your bank account," he said. "Trust that you can do this, and that it will be there for you."

A few days later, I received a check and beautiful note in the mail. It included another lesson about how to find more faith in myself and a Higher Power. I leaned into his guidance. What I was doing wasn't working—so I was willing to try anything.

As the months went by, I found my zone. Slowly, more clients started to come in. The money began flowing as I'd hoped it would. My worries started to lessen, and I started trusting myself and my decisions again. I never needed to ask for another check—but I knew that it was there if I needed it, and that meant just as much.

Uncle John and I continued our conversations on and off for some time. His love and support meant the world to me. With his help, I found my way to a place of ease and certainty. I turned my ship around, and realized that I was not, and had never been, a failure—not to my clients, not to my family, and not to myself. I *hadn't* been wrong to leave my job: I was living my purpose. The Universe just needed some time to catch up with my decisions—and to show me what real faith was.

During this time, I also learned how to communicate with angels, spirit guides, and the Universe (he never minded that I don't call it God). And through it all, my uncle, my guardian angel, was there whenever I needed him.

In July of 2018, Uncle John passed away. As I was driving from Rhode Island to New Jersey to be with him in his last moments, I remember feeling a strong desire to be there for him as he'd been there for me. And I was.

After he passed, I didn't know how to process his loss. I was relieved that he was no longer suffering, and that he'd been reunited with his parents, his brother, and the many people he'd loved who had passed before him. And yet, I missed him, and I felt adrift without our conversations to keep me grounded.

Then, I started seeing the cardinals.

Whenever I found myself needing our connection, Uncle John would send me a red-breasted cardinal. They would show up in my yard, in trees as I drove, or even on social media. In 2020, when so many businesses imploded due to the pandemic, I continued to ask for his wisdom—and the cardinals would always reappear to show me I was on the right path.

Even as I write this, there's a particularly bright-breasted cardinal hanging out on the dogwood tree outside my window. I know Uncle John is here, just checking on me, and letting me know that it's all okay.

Finding faith in yourself and trusting your path is a process that takes practice. Even when you can't find enough belief in yourself to fill a teacup, try to have faith in the process. More, remember that you don't have to go it alone. We all need help from others—in this life, and beyond. Don't hold back from asking. Don't hold the weight of your worry and fear alone. Love, kindness, and the answers you seek are out there, if you are only brave enough to ask.

THE TRUE SHAPE
OF SUCCESS

RENÉE POIRIER

WHAT DOES IT MEAN to be successful?

To a young girl living in suburbia, it means being accepted into a big-name college. To a young athlete, it means being awarded an athletic scholarship at the Division One level. To the daughter of parents who constantly fought about money, it means achieving financial comfort and independence. My definition of success has changed almost annually throughout the last decade of my life, with each year marking a new milestone.

Make the honor roll? Make the varsity softball team as a freshman? Become team captain? *Check.*

Get recruited to play softball at West Point? Throw a no-hitter? Become team captain, again? *Check.*

Graduate college with no debt? Commission as a Second Lieutenant in the United States Army? Pay off my car? Travel around the world on my own?

Check, check, check, check.

I did not have much external pressure to accomplish these things, but I had expectations of myself to live an impressive life of recognition and financial comfort. I set and then accomplished each one of these goals to keep me moving on the path to my shallow destination. Never being satisfied no matter how far I progressed, I put incredible pressure on myself to continue achieving at higher and higher levels. I craved the temporary feeling of success, with the hopes that maybe, just maybe, one of my accomplishments would leave me feeling like I achieved the overarching goal of an impressive life. Meanwhile, I was desperately searching for some semblance of purpose.

In a suburban Massachusetts small town, expectations are clear-cut. You get good grades, stay out of trouble, and get into college. The higher the grades, the better. The more recognizable the school's name, the more compliments on your acceptance. Not only will your family be proud of you, but practically the whole town will be. Your neighbors, your friends' parents, and even your brother's friends' parents will congratulate you when you run into them at the grocery store or the local Target.

My middle school softball coach asked me if I had ever heard of the U.S. Military Academy at West Point. At the time I hadn't, but I quickly began my research. There were a few things that grabbed my attention.

First: it's ranked the top public college in the United States by Forbes. Second: it would be tuition-free for me; I'd pay for tuition with Army service time as opposed to student loans. Third: they have Division One softball. Fourth: after graduation, I'd have a guaranteed well-paid job, plus I could get stationed anywhere and experience life outside of Massachusetts. Fifth: I would have two years of school to test the waters before deciding what I want to major in.

And finally, attending West Point would assure me I would not be stuck working some nine-to-five job. I would be a part of something greater than myself, where I could make a difference.

My next goal was identified. I immediately set about executing next steps.

Then I faced my first bout of failure. The most prominent travel team in the area did not want me.

This team was known for its nationwide travel schedule and high-caliber college recruitments. As a fifteen-year-old girl with sky-high dreams of playing college softball, I thought this team would give me the best odds to achieve that dream. Were there other travel team options? Absolutely. But by then, my ego was hurt.

This was my first taste of major failure. Up until this point, I'd achieved every goal I'd ever set. This door slammed in my face, and I was devastated.

I always strove for the best. The most renowned or prestigious option was what defined success for me. Though it was only through a travel softball team organization, being told I was "not good enough" for the first time in my life was a wake-up call that would offer lasting lessons.

After swallowing my pride and realizing that getting recruited to West Point was just as obtainable on other travel teams, I joined a team that was a great fit, where I made a lot of friends and met a couple of lasting mentors. And, by my junior year, I was committed to playing softball at West Point.

I was so excited to get the acceptance call that I ran around my house, jumping up and down while still on the phone. I'd made it happen. I was setting myself up for success both personally and financially. I would have no student loans and a guaranteed job with complete medical care coverage. I was headed toward my life goals of recognition and financial stability, and every adult I encountered was sure to remind me of it with their congratulations.

My time at West Point was challenging. Like most other cadets, my biggest struggle was the Cadet Basic Training—also referred to as "Beast." The training occurred the summer before our freshman year at the Academy; its completion was a requirement to even be considered a cadet.

To survive the first half of Beast, you had to be at least decent at two basic tasks.

The first was to run. We ran every morning in formation. For anyone who grew up playing softball, you know we are not the best runners. I fell out of every single run.

The second task was to memorize the knowledge book. On the first day, Reception Day, they give you a paper book small enough to fit in the back pocket of your baggy wool uniform pants. It is filled with facts about the Academy and the Army that you are required to memorize. The knowledge includes anything from the ranks of non-commissioned officers (very important) to the number of lights in Cullum Hall (maybe a little less important). I could not get this knowledge to stick in my brain. When the cadre came around to ask me what knowledge I had prepared to recite verbatim, it was usually a sad attempt at the shortest entry in the section. Saying, "Nothing" was not an option. My feeling of inadequacy was overwhelming. I did not feel like I belonged in that school, and some of the cadre agreed.

The cadre was made up of the Academy's juniors and seniors, so their disapproval was extremely disheartening. I was being rejected by the pack, unable to be accepted as one of their own. A sense of failure overtook me in the same way it did when I got cut from the travel softball team. I started to question my ability to succeed at this next milestone. So many people from back home were proud of me; the thought of letting them down was painful.

One day at the range, I was told by one squad leader to line up at lane ten, after another had told me to go to lane eleven only five minutes prior. I could see the disappointment in the eyes of the squad who told me to go to lane eleven when I chose instead to go to lane ten. Well, I got a whole lot more than disappointed eyes: that squad leader told me on that August day that I would never make it to graduation.

The worst part was, I completely believed her. I doubted my ability to make it past the summer training to the academic year, and my ability to make it beyond that to graduation.

Not once during that first summer at the Academy did I think about my ability to be a successful Lieutenant in the US Army. I later learned that lack of foresight is not uncommon. Something special about the Academy is the structure of increasing leadership. My freshman year was all about learning how to follow. It was accepted that you could only learn to lead once you understood how to follow. As you reach your sophomore year, you become responsible for mentoring one freshman. You are their team leader. I learned that, as a leader, their failure is my failure. I could have better prepared them in some way. As you become a junior and senior, you become a leader of more cadets, and the leadership lessons continue to flow.

As I progressed year to year through my career at West Point, I became progressively more successful. During my freshman year, I received Cs and accepted that at this smart school I was an average student—a large fish in an ocean of sharks. By the time I reached my senior year, I was getting Bs, with a couple of As.

Apparently, I began to believe in myself a little too late.

My softball career moved in the opposite direction. I started super strong. I had an extremely close bond with my pitching coach and broke multiple school and league records in my freshman and sophomore years. Once he left, my performance leveled out and I was no longer a force to fear in the league.

In the end, through the rise and fall of both my academic and athletic performances, I graduated from West Point with the most confidence I'd ever known. Everything seemed to be coming together. I learned that I am capable of a whole lot more than I thought.

I went to West Point for the selfish reasons I listed earlier—but by the end of my time there, I was truly inspired to serve my country and felt prepared to be the best possible leader for my future soldiers. My physical fitness was at its peak, and I was eager to begin a fruitful career in the Army.

That is not to say I wasn't intimidated by the fact that I would soon be leading a group of soldiers—husbands, fathers, wives, mothers, sons, and daughters. I did not take the responsibility lightly. My time as a platoon leader came with unique challenges but also a lot of inspiration. I was granted a platoon of soldiers who were motivated to get better both individually, furthering their careers, and as a team, to accomplish tasks. Their efforts motivated me to be the best leader I could be for them, and lead by example.

West Point prepared me well to prioritize tasks and plan training exercises efficiently, yet my favorite part of the job was getting to work with people from all corners of the nation and all types of backgrounds. It was an honor to lead soldiers, more than I expected it would be as a cadet. I was excited about my platoon's upcoming gunnery and the next great opportunity I knew the Army would provide me.

Two and a half years after graduation, my Army officer glide path came to a screeching halt. I woke up to being sexually assaulted by someone I considered to be my best friend in the unit. At that moment, I felt my soul leave my body. I felt like a piece of meat being used only for a man's pleasure.

After the assault, my mental health plummeted. I had to check the locks on my doors three or four times before going up to bed, and then lock my bedroom door as well. I could not leave my house without having trouble breathing, terrified of running into my attacker. I was constantly looking in my rearview mirror for fear of being followed. I moved to the other side of the city, hoping to feel slightly safer, but it didn't help. My bouts of depression were extremely dark. After months of trying to cope and being told by doctors and therapists that I was "doing all the right things" to help myself get to a better place, I felt worse than ever.

The pain began to feel permanent—and that is when it became unbearable.

I turned to self-harm, cutting, out of desperation to feel anything other than the pain and fear, and to punish myself for not getting better despite my best efforts and those of my therapists. I wasn't intentionally digging for a vein, but I wasn't worried about hitting one either. I had no passion for life. I felt alone, empty, and completely broken. It did not feel like my pain would ever end.

Immediately after the attack, I decided against reporting anything to our command team. I did not want to go through the long legal process. At that time, I didn't want my "best friend" to get in trouble, and I didn't want his wife or newborn daughter to suffer the knowledge of his cruelty. I did not feel like *my* pain counted. I did not feel worthy of the battle to come.

The turning point for me was when I began to think about all the teenage girls I had (and still have) the pleasure of coaching in softball. I asked myself, *What would you do if one of those girls came to you after experiencing a similar trauma, and asked you for advice?*

My immediate answer was, *I would encourage her to stand up for herself. Renée, how can you ask a young girl to do something you are unwilling to do yourself?*

It was then that I decided to report the attack.

At that moment, I realized I would not only be standing up for myself, I would be standing up for all the other women and girls who do not feel worthy either. I stood up for the women who know from experience that 70 percent of defendants in sexual assault cases are not found guilty. The girls that I coach now, and will coach in the future, deserve to have a face they know who has fought the pain and challenged those percentages because she believed in herself more than she believed in numbers.

That is my current definition of success—that I believe in myself more than I believe in statistics.

While I was treading water throughout the process of recovery, just trying to keep afloat, I had no perspective. I could not even see my hand two feet in front of me. Circling back, I realized two things that never crossed my mind when I was at my lowest point. When I was admitted to a mental health hospital, I did not once think about financial comfort or recognition. Those two things—the things I'd considered my guiding lights throughout my teenage years—were not even passing thoughts when I confronted the brutally honest question of whether I wanted to continue to live on this earth.

Instead, I thought about the people I love. I did not want to miss out on supporting them through their accomplishments and milestones. The love we share helped me recognize all there still is to live for, and all the events that are still worth celebrating. I am blessed to have my family. They have been so supportive throughout my recovery process, and allow me to be honest about my progress. I used to think I had to put up a strong front so that I wouldn't worry anybody, but that left me in a very lonely place. I found that being honest with my loved ones about what I am going through has allowed me to reconnect with my family members in a way that I had been missing out on for a long time. Our family relationships are stronger than ever, and my soul has begun to ignite again.

Once my inner world felt more stable, I began to think about my purpose. I knew that if I was going to find true joy again on this earth, and not end up back where I had been, I was going to have to discover my true purpose, something that kept my soul on fire and excited for the next day. I began to think about what truly made me happy and where I felt I was filling a void in the world, leaving an impact in a space that needed to be filled. I still have not come to a definitive answer around all that my purpose may include, but I have arrived at an understanding of the overall uniqueness of my being.

That discovery is what led me to contribute to *Born to Rise*. I love coaching and sharing the lessons I have learned with younger generations, but I know I also have so much more to give outside the sport of softball. There is a creative side of me begging to come out that has laid dormant for many years. I have begun this path of discovery, back home in Massachusetts, surrounded by the people I love. I am excited to take a chance on myself and pursue opportunities in multiple dimensions so that I may create the most I can possibly offer this world.

Only a few years ago, I thought titles and accolades could make me successful. I traveled around the country and to places all over the world, all to confirm that my place was back home with those I love and trust the most. The ironic thing is, I have never felt more successful. My new guiding light is to leave a powerfully positive impact on others that outlasts my time with them—a time that I vow not to conclude of my own accord.

THE SAFE PLACE WITHIN

DOMINEY DREW

LIKE SO MANY HUMANS on this planet, life was a struggle for me. And, like so many humans on this planet, I was unintentionally making it so—although I had no idea this was the case until later in life, when it was confirmed to me beyond a shadow of a doubt.

The realization that I—that we, humans—create our reality in every aspect was, well, shocking, and I initially responded with disbelief. It took twenty-five years of life experience (mine, and my clients' as well) to get to me accept this counterintuitive perspective as reality, but that acceptance was the most transformative and empowering shift I have ever made in my life.

***

I didn't have an extreme or violent upbringing. I was loved by my parents, always fed, watered, and educated. Up until I was seven years old, I remained blissfully unaware that conflict existed in the world beyond my siblings being mean to me (always their fault, of course; I was an angel).

When I was seven, my father left for the arms of another woman, shattering our cohesive family unit and introducing me to the new reality that life wasn't as safe as I'd always believed.

From my perspective, the container upon which I'd relied for my safety, and which I'd assumed was unbreakable, had cracked, leaving me feeling abandoned and unsure of myself. From my seven-year-old perspective, the situation felt like life or death.

As children, we all experience a kind of wounding. Not necessarily from a "trauma" the way our adult minds might define it, but from a moment when we as children *perceive* our lives as threatened, which is why woundings can result from events that don't actually risk our physical lives. When this event occurs, the child draws a conclusion about life, herself, or others, that she then *generalizes* to the entire world. These conclusions lodge deep in the subconscious, and take the form of broad, overarching statements such as:

"The world is unsafe."

"Men can't be trusted."

"People will leave me."

"I am not enough."

When my father left and my mother entered a two-year depression as a result, I experienced my childhood wounding and was forever changed.

My conclusion was: "It is not safe to be me."

With that subconscious assumption firmly in place, I entered a state of near-constant inauthenticity that continued for the next twenty years. It took many forms: people pleasing, fear of confrontation, rejection of self, judgment of others, body dysmorphia, negative self-talk, depression, and anxiety, to name a few.

***

During the ensuing four years of divorce proceedings, I saw several child therapists. One day, as we sat in a nondescript room in Santa Barbara, California, I remember one of them asking me:

"Who do you want to live with, your mother or your father?"

I will never forget that question.

That was the moment I split in two.

I can't express the *tearing* I experienced in response to her words. I felt it on levels I didn't know I had—a deep, visceral rending that was real in a way I'd never known. Suddenly, I couldn't feel myself. I didn't know what I wanted, or who I was. I was unsure. I doubted myself.

That pattern of self-doubt continued for the next two decades until I had delved deeply enough into myself to recognize and heal it.

In that therapist's office, I was faced with an impossible situation. Choosing one parent over the other felt so wrong, and yet there was no way out. It was like being squeezed through the eye of a needle. I was forced into an impossible scenario, and without realizing it, I split, froze, and disconnected from myself, imperceptibly and nearly irrevocably.

It wasn't until I was nineteen years old that I began to understand any of this. By then, I'd already struggled with severe depression for several years. I'd finally found a medication that helped somewhat, but no drug solves the underlying problem, so I searched for real answers. My continued anguish led me to a weekend workshop at a retreat center in Virginia. It was in a methodology called Pathwork, and in one weekend I transformed more than I thought humanly possible. I was hooked.

This experience prompted a decades-long journey to discover who I really was. For the next four years, I studied at a Pathwork school, then at an energy healing school for another four years, then I completed a Master's degree. Each training was more intensive than the last, inviting me over and over again to face the real, underlying reality of life, others, and myself, that I had hidden from since childhood.

Gradually, I found the words and located each exact moment when I had split from myself, and brought my adult, conscious awareness to it. This was the magic. The ability to see, with one's conscious, adult perspective, what one had mistakenly assumed to be true as a child is the source of human growth. It is the technique I used to regain my sense of self and take true ownership of my life, and it is the technique I use to help my clients do the same.

Ultimately, it's the process of attaining enlightenment.

***

Over the years, I discovered ever more layers of belief and assumption, each time stepping more fully into myself, gaining strength, balance, and confidence. As I did so, my relationship with life began to change.

I had always struggled against life. Only it didn't feel that way. It felt more like life was against me, that if I stopped fighting, it would swallow me up and I would disappear. It never occurred to me to not fight. I'd developed an unconscious belief that if I didn't force things to happen, nothing would happen. I believed that if I didn't control or *make* life be what I wanted, I would not be okay.

It is not safe to be me ...

One day in year three of healing school, I stood by a tall glass window, the Austrian mountains looming outside, still and mysterious. As a class, we were giving each other energy healings, and I stood beside my classmate/client who lay in front of me. As I worked on her, I suddenly glimpsed a fork in the road ahead of me. I saw a path forward that was effortless—an action or movement I could do in this healing that was simple, and unforced. Simultaneously, I saw another option—an action that would require a push from me. I was far more attracted to the forcing—it was familiar, I knew that path of life, and I trusted it. It was uncomfortable but safe.

At that moment, I saw my pattern, my inclination not to be trapped by struggle, but to *choose* it! The moment I perceived this, I recognized the belief I carried around it: somewhere, deep in my system, I confused struggle with life force; I linked fighting, drama, and forcing with being alive.

Wow! *No wonder* I continued to choose to struggle! No wonder I fought for it, felt attracted to it, and continued subconsciously to go down paths that hurt. Pain was one thing. Not living at all was far worse.

What followed was a massive shift in my perception and my life. Over the next few years, I began to explore and untangle my relationship with effort, control, and forcing things to be. Gradually, as I realized life might not depend completely upon my control, my constantly anxious system began to relax. I grew more comfortable simply allowing life, and other people, to be as they are.

Throughout this time, I started to give myself permission to stop taking responsibility for other people's life experiences, to allow them to take their path and really know that not only are they strong enough to handle it, but that it is their sacred right to do so.

In college, I had an experience that changed my perspective, and thus who I was, forever. I was in my dorm room, on the phone with my mother, walking around in circles as I often do on phone calls. I had just broken up with my boyfriend, and I was distraught. The relationship needed to end for many reasons, but the amount of pain I felt as a result of causing pain to another (which was how I saw leaving my ex) was intolerable. It was almost enough to make me want to stay in the dead-end relationship, just to avoid hurting him.

I described to my mother how I felt breaking this young man's heart: "It's like putting my bare hand on a piece of freshly split wood, pressing down, and running my hand along the grain as thousands of splinters pierce my skin."

Tears flowed. She gave time for the wave of emotion to move through me, and when I was ready to receive, she spoke: "It's neither your job nor your right to control the life experience of another."

Everything stopped.

I felt my world shifting. I'd never thought about it this way. I was a people pleaser; I wanted to fix everyone and everything, and honestly, subconsciously I thought I *had* to. On some level, I thought it was my job. The realization that not only was it not my job, it wasn't even my *right*, rocked me. I thought I was helping, and I suddenly saw that my selfless love was actually selfish control.

What I'd meant as support was actually invading and controlling his life experience. It was not to be kind, as I'd originally thought, but actually to protect myself from the pain *I felt* at seeing his pain. My attempt to protect him from pain was a front to avoid tolerating my own discomfort.

I was trying to protect my ex from pain, but what right had I to do such a thing? Pain is a natural and powerful part of life. How we respond to it is how we create ourselves and determine who we are and who we want to become. I would never trade the pain I've experienced in my life. Without it, I would not have risen.

Additionally, to try to keep him from feeling pain, I indicated to him that he couldn't handle it. That I, the strong one, would manage and moderate his feelings based on what I decided he was capable of experiencing. Without even meaning to, I was infantilizing the man I had loved. I disrespected him, cut him off at the knees, and positioned myself as capable, and him as weak.

As these realizations crashed around me, my view of myself, and thus who I was, began to shift. I had an image of myself as kind, selfless, loving, and giving. And in many ways, I was that person. But at this moment, I was twisting those gifts into self-protection, because I was scared, distorting my core qualities as a psychological defense, to avoid the perceived pain—the pain of seeing humans hurt. Wanting to *fix* another person looked like kindness, but was actually controlling.

A beautiful realization came to me: if you aren't strong enough to tolerate the pain of others, how can you heal them?

***

My addiction to struggle, once identified, transformed quickly. I released more and more control, faced more and more fears, and rose, ever higher, into ease and flow.

At one point, I stepped completely into effortlessness and for several years I existed in a kind of semi-enlightenment. My default state became not only accepting that things are the way they are but truly loving how they are!

They are perfect.

Life is perfect.

You are perfect.

I am perfect.

This new state of acceptance and surrender doesn't mean I don't enact change in the world—in fact, quite the opposite. However, I no longer try to enact change from a place of needing to "fix" other people, avoiding what is, fearing for others, or needing to be right. Instead, I enact change because it brings me joy. I invest in paradigm-shifting sustainability tech, speak on large stages to create inspiration, facilitate powerful personal transformation, and most gloriously, teach people how to live lives of effortless freedom and joy.

In doing so I am elevating and living in alignment with my highest purpose.

For me, every day is effortless.

I used to believe that it was not safe to be me. The day I realized that safety is created within me was the day I began to rise.

Rise into

FREEDOM

THE WORLD WAS NEVER DEAF

KIM HAYES & JULIANA HAYES

SO MANY LABELS can be applied to me: female, a child of divorce, poor, victim, abandoned, bereaved, gay, bisexual. A label is an abstract concept in sociology used to group people together based on perceived or held identity. Labels are a mode of identifying social groups. Labels can create a sense of community, but they can also be used to separate individuals and groups from mainstream society in a damaging way. Throughout our lives, people attach labels to us, and those labels reflect and affect how others think about our identities as well as how we think about ourselves.

Having a label is like trying to dance along a tightrope. Gracefully leaping in between the black and the white of societal expectations, while still desperately grasping for comfort in the gray areas.

The whispers of a fulfilling future convince you to keep up with the ever-changing choreography that time presents, even though anxiety rips through your stomach and anchors you to the reality of the ground beneath the slender rope. The hope of one day being able to leap off the shaking rope encourages you to disregard your scarred body and recovering mind. The day you can no longer bring yourself to dance initializes your long downfall. Even as you fall, the solace of finally finding that gray area causes you to trust gravity and just close your eyes. You know that the dance is finally over.

***

At only nineteen years old, so many possibilities were thundering and echoing throughout my brain. Would I be accepted if I told my mom? Would I be loved? Or worse, could I be rejected? My hands trembled as I clenched my blanket, tears falling in rebellion against my wishes. The air of all the unspoken expectations in my house swirled around in my head and threatened to keep pushing me over until I had lived my whole life on my knees.

Although the fatal car accident that took my brother's life occurred five years previously, only now could I sense the quiet voice of stability finally regained in my household. The quiet voice that I now threatened to silence with the deafening sound of my truth. Would this be the axe to the fragile sense of normalcy we had achieved?

Could I possibly disappoint or fail my mother more than life already had? But I had to say it. There was no other choice. Holding back my truth was lying to myself, telling myself I should be something different than who I am.

My truth is, I am gay.

The notion that I could be different came at the age of five, when I was violated and had my innocence taken away from me. When the label of *victim* should have been given to me, a memento to my trauma and pain. Yet, never was the word even uttered. I had to move forward while my entire world was stripped of light and color and sound. I couldn't talk about it. The only therapy or closure I received was the subtle yet agonizing comfort of acknowledgment. My family knew what had happened; they recognized that my senses had been stripped away and discarded like trash you find on the sidewalk. When I asked my mother and brothers if I had imagined what happened to me, they gave me a torturous head-shake of disagreement.

I didn't have the gift of growing up in an age where we are encouraged to share our truth, encouraged to heal and grow and demand from the world what it is we truly deserve. No, we kept quiet and moved on. What good would a label do me if no one can hear it? If the whole world is deaf, why should I scream? After all, a label is just a word.

***

My coming out marked the next point on the timeline dating my animosity toward labels. I remember the conversation in pieces. It wasn't the way I wanted it to happen. Nor the way I imagined all the possibilities of how I was going to sit her down and tell her. Rather, it was in a burst of emotion. I cried for weeks leading up to this moment. Mom had asked me so many times, "What's wrong?" But I couldn't bring myself to tell her.

That day though … that day was different.

Yet again, she asked me, "Kimmy, what's wrong?"

I found my voice for the first time in my life, and yelled, "Mom, I'm gay!"

Every bit of air was sucked out of the room, but somehow there was still enough oxygen for her to let out a single, exasperated breath.

"*What*?" Mom's expression was like she was looking at a person who committed a murder. A person who kidnapped a child. A person who had committed a heinous crime. It was not the face of a mother looking at her child.

We sat in that breathlessness for a couple more minutes. I was careful not to move as it would disturb the warped sense of peace. Careful not to make a single sound that would disrupt her processing of my statement.

The misshapen reality was broken as she mumbled to herself, a panicked expression masking her face. Her tears fell silently as she walked away from me—away from us, and everything our relationship had been.

I wish I could have relished those moments of silence for just a little while longer.

"Mom, can we talk about this?" I quickly moved from my bed and followed her as she staggered into our living room. Mom was walking towards the hutch. Everything else in our house was relatively ordinary, except for the items in that hutch. It was filled with Japanese dolls she had collected over the years, some of her most prized possessions. Her hand was shaking as she reached for one doll in particular.

"Mom, please stop. Just … sit down."

She began to sob loudly as she held the doll I had bought her for Christmas. I had spent my entire summer saving up for it. It was unique in its beauty, with dark hair and red painted on the cheeks to give a rosy expression. Mom's sadness turned to rage as she took the beautiful doll and smashed it against our cluttered table. I screamed at her to stop. Her words were indecipherable as she took this gift and destroyed it in front of me. The hoarded memorabilia and meaningless decorative pieces on our table were becoming clouded in the dust of the doll. I sat there, now sobbing uncontrollably.

"I didn't mean it, Mom. Please, just *stop*!"

"How could this happen to me?" she said, her hand bleeding from the shattered pieces of the doll. I watched helplessly as she devolved further into her childlike tantrum. Usually, I was an expert in handling her spouts of rage; ever since my brother's death, I had developed a doctorate in mediation. After his death, a small part of her had gone missing, as if she too had died in his car that day. I had learned the ability to judge whether she would be in a good mood or a bad one by the simple flinch of her eyebrow. Whether or not she would be my kind, loving mother, or someone else. That day, nothing could calm her.

She ran to her bedroom and closed the door. I followed her, but even before I turned the knob, I knew it was locked. My tears fell onto the cold metal as I kept trying to push through, but my hands kept slipping.

"Mom, let me in."

I heard her dialing the phone. "Kimmy is killing me, Mom. She's killing me."

The door cracked open just enough for my mother to thrust the phone at me; as I put the receiver to my ear, I could hear my sweet grandmother screaming at me, saying how I had disappointed our family. She disowned me, my last name now added to the list of words taken from me. My mother snatched the phone back from me and the door slammed once again. My words became more and more desperate as I heard the distinct sound of pills dropping on the floor. *No. No, no, no, no. This isn't happening.*

"Mom, *please!*" I banged on the door, frantic. Eventually, the door opened. I dragged her into the car and drove her to the emergency room.

The label "gay" was not worth this.

***

I never could have imagined the impact a label would have on my life that day—that I would have to push past and silence any feelings about that interaction with my mom and continue to help her despite her estrangement from my identity.

The gift of time has granted me reflection and a clear view of the starting point when my adversity to labels began. A map of all the life events that conglomerated into my negative disposition toward self-identifiers.

The moment I set sail was my failed coming out story, though the ocean would drown more and more of myself until all my pride was washed away. My life has consisted of not one Titanic, but many. When I was twenty-one and newly enlisted in the Navy, I was faced with the question of my sexuality and the hot breath of the recruiter down my neck, struggling not to seem flustered. At twenty-five, when my oldest daughter needed medical care, I was forced to sit and watch, unable to help due to a law refuting my motherhood. At that time, same sex couples were not allowed to adopt, so my wife, her biological mother, was the only one allowed to make medical decisions for her.

At twenty-eight, I was refused the right of marriage because I had found my happily ever after not in a prince, but a princess.

Eventually, my adversity began its metamorphosis into acceptance.

***

I stood in front of the mirror, contemplating whether or not I liked my outfit for dinner. I had picked out a red button-up blouse with black slacks and even applied a dash of concealer, though makeup was never something I was dexterous with. My wife Michelle, my daughter Juliana, and I were going out for dinner for our anniversary, so I wanted to look decent. I took a breath, brushed out my hair once more for good measure, and met my family in the living room to drive to the restaurant.

The car ride was standard for our family: my wife was silent, focusing on driving, and my now-teenage daughter was absorbed in whatever novel media outlet she was currently consuming. Neither of them seemed interested in conversation, so I watched the trees pass by as we approached our location.

As we took our seats in the back corner of the restaurant, I gave Juliana the look to put her phone down. Although a little annoyed, she complied.

"If I have to, you guys should too," she said, with a defiant look in her eye.

This seemed fair, so I stacked my phone top of hers, and nudged Michelle under the table to do the same.

"I just have a couple of emails to send—one second." This was often her rebuttal to my daughter's efforts.

Instead of refuting her, Juliana and I both talked about our days—

or rather, she rambled on about hers, and I listened. She gave a detailed description of each class, and though I was not fully attentive, my ears perked as she described a discussion from her history class.

"Can you believe they said that labels don't matter? I mean, *seriously*?"

Though she seemed proud in the assertion of her opinion, I've never been one to hold back my thoughts. "Well, do they really?"

Juliana's face filled with shock as she processed what I said. My wife remained absorbed in her technology. "Of course they do! I mean, people need them for a sense of community."

"I understand that, but your generation seems so obsessed with them. Why do we *need* to have a label?"

My wife finally looked up from her phone and, after taking a sip of water, decided to join in. "I think things were easier in the old days. More people get hurt now because of labels."

Juliana gave her a look of frustration, as their views often differed. "You think it was better when people couldn't even express themselves?"

I could see this ending badly and cursed myself for even continuing the line of conversation. Michelle was obviously annoyed, as I don't think that was how she meant her statement to be heard, but even I had to disagree with her.

"I have to agree with Juliana here. Things were not better when we were kids."

"Sorry for having an opinion." She gave a defeated sigh and returned to her phone. I felt bad because that wasn't my intention, but had to return my attention to my daughter, as she was demanding an explanation.

"I'm just saying," I began, "that I don't understand why your generation cares so much about labels."

"It's not that we *need* to have them. It's that having them can give some kind of comfort in this screwed-up world. You know how it feels to be different. Imagine if, when you were younger, you had an outlet and a community who shared your exact struggles. *That's* why my generation cares about labels."

There were times I felt very alone and questioned the reason for my existence. Having a sense of community may have helped me with my self-confidence and value. Being part of a community could have had a long-term positive impact. But I don't look back on life and have regrets. I believe we are put on the path we are meant to travel.

Our food finally came, and I ended the conversation. Not because I disagreed or couldn't think of something to say, but because I resonated with my daughter's words more than I even realized.

As I lay in bed that night, I thought about what she'd said and truly tried to imagine what having the ability to talk to someone would have done for me in all my moments of trauma. I recognized that this could mark a turning point for me.

My mind went to the lyrics of a song Juliana had written. *You walk in and protect me / You're my walls from the outside.*

I am bisexual. I am in a same-sex marriage. I am a woman. I am a daughter. I am a sister. I am an aunt. I am a spouse. I am a boss. I was a victim. I am a survivor. I am a mom of two beautiful daughters who have given me the courage and strength to share my story.

I have been inspired to take this leap and share my story by watching my children push forward in life. If there is fear, they never let it stop them, as I did. We all feel fear, but it's not an excuse for inaction.

When I feel at risk of being erased, I am reminded that no label or words can do that. My story didn't end because of the trauma I experienced. I'm not stuck in those awful moments just because the labels acknowledge that they happened.

I hope that in my pain others can heal—that my story can provide a basis for other women to overcome, thrive, and succeed. I am no longer silent; I am able to speak my truth and I know that I have people who will support me as I continue on this journey.

In actuality, the world was never deaf, it was just waiting for me to ask for help.

THE CASE FOR LETTING GO

JESS SPINO

THERE'S SOMETHING LIBERATING about hitting rock bottom. Because when you're looking up from the gutter and wondering how the hell you got there, there's literally nothing left to do but claw your way back out.

That was the start of 2020 for me, and I know you're thinking, "Yeah, well, you and everyone else," but it's not for the reasons you think. See, toward the end of 2019, my husband of fifteen years—my Mikey, my best friend, my rock, and the Aquarius to my Leo—got sick. What started with some hip pain graduated to a limp, and by January of 2020, he was unable to get out of bed unassisted or walk without a cane. My healthy, athletic man was on medical leave from work because he was flat on his back most days, either crying or yelling in anger at this mystery illness.

I found myself in a less-than-ideal position as well, also flat on my back, but in the figurative sense. I was a shell of who I had been just three years earlier—the spunky, ass-kicking organizational master with a wicked sense of humor and style, two prestigious degrees, and a resumé as long as my arm. I'd been working as the right hand to a successful business coach, and the two of us had built her empire from $100,000 in annual revenue to over $4 million in just three years. What had started as an administrative support position to a solopreneur quickly grew to a COO role for a team of twenty and a roster of over 1,000 clients from around the world.

Sounds pretty great, right?

I was talented, and on paper, everything was perfect. In the beginning, I pinched myself daily. I loved being valued as an integral member of the team, and I got constant reinforcement by being told that nobody did it better than me. My boss showed her appreciation by flying me around the world to retreats and events where we partied with celebrities, walked red carpets, and shopped like millionaires. Friend, it was the stuff dreams are made of.

But in teeny, tiny increments, I started exchanging everything that was dear to me for this other, star-studded life—a life I had never known I wanted (and honestly, still wasn't sure I even did). Work took precedence over everything. I took urgent calls during family parties and analyzed passive-aggressive text threads during my daughter's dance recitals. I prided myself on being the "Fixer," the "I've Got It Girl," and I couldn't let any cracks show.

The trade-off came so slowly that I didn't even notice I was carrying the weight of *All. The. Things.* I took on more and more at work—and my boss supported my shaky hands just enough to steady the blocks I was precariously placing on top of my heightening tower, with no regard for the fact that its center was hollow.

In me, my boss had the perfect Yes Woman. Somehow, I felt unworthy of it all, and also deeply indebted to her for the lifestyle I was enjoying. I was treading water, desperately trying to stay afloat, but secretly wishing the current would sweep me under so I didn't have to endure one more day. I was exhausted, and despite everything I was doing, I still had the nagging feeling that it wasn't enough.

In the meantime, mysterious illnesses of my own started cropping up—vertigo, digestive issues, rashes—and I'd wake up in a panic most nights, disoriented and groping for my phone. I fantasized about being hospitalized, but just long enough so I had a good excuse to rest. Two different doctors told me that my symptoms were the result of stress and overworking, which I poo-pooed until a time study revealed I had logged fifty-six hours of work during a holiday week.

All along, my husband had been telling me I was like a battered wife, constantly running back to an existence that left me broken, but I couldn't see it. There was always an excuse that it was just "this one time," or some small shiny thing that made the hard work seem momentarily worth it.

There was also the fear. The paralyzing, knot-in-my-stomach, heart-in-my-throat terror that I'd let my boss down and be the subject of her next Zoom call diatribe. My coworkers would watch in silent relief that it was me being humiliated instead of them this time, and I couldn't blame them for not intervening; I'd been in their shoes before.

I'd finally been pushed to my limits enough times that I stood up to my boss and told her how unhappy I had become. The truth tumbled from my lips so fast that I couldn't catch it. I told her about the doctors' visits, the overworking, and about feeling pulled toward more. She was cold and silent, but fury blazed in her eyes. Her mouth twisted into a mocking smile and she said nothing, ending our meeting early and leaving me to deal with the anticipation of the punishment I expected I would endure.

Almost two weeks went by after that conversation, and we never spoke about it again. I was desperate for a confrontation so it could be over, but I was also used to being stonewalled. During that time, her communications with me were direct, polite, chillingly unemotional, and utterly agonizing. Then, one day, my worst fear came true, and I saw my destiny there in front of me in black and white.

As I had predicted, on a video call in front of my coworkers and several clients, she taunted me—criticizing everything I'd worked so hard for, for her! I sat stunned, my eyes glazing over as shame rose in my cheeks. And just like that, I realized how little the difference I thought I was making mattered to her. I was making the ultimate sacrifice of my time, my health, my freedom, and my family—my entire identity—for someone who thought I was disposable.

The harsh reality finally hit me as I turned off my camera. I didn't want to be the woman my girls told stories about as adults—the detached, distant mom who bought them stuff in exchange for her time and attention. And I definitely wouldn't leave my husband a young widower, especially in the condition he was in.

I did what any desperate woman would do. Enough was enough, and the longer I stayed at this job that beat me into the ground, the more I identified with it as who I was. And I didn't want to be that person anymore. I made the decision to break free and write my own ending, the first words of which were my resignation letter. And with that, I jumped into nothingness without any idea where I would land.

I had no plan, no clue what I would do. I had nothing but two preteen daughters, a hefty mortgage payment, and a furloughed husband whose words reminded me of the old me (the real me!) and carried me through as they rang in my head: *"If we ever get in some shit, you're the one who is going to get us out."*

Oddly enough, it was what I *didn't* do that got us out of the proverbial shit we were in. For once in my life, I surrendered control. I built my wings as I fell, and I trusted that they'd be ready to lift me before I hit the ground. I centered my life around what *my* priorities were, not anyone else's. As a woman who was used to measuring her worth by her ability to fix things, for once, simply being present was the cure. I had to really be there, in the moment, sometimes not doing anything but lying on our family room floor with Mike, holding space for him to just feel, without saying a word. Syncing our breaths and heartbeats and knowing that the future was not mine to dictate.

I had to get present and tune back in to the independent, straight-shooting me again, reclaiming the identity that those who truly knew and loved me had always seen. The wounds were deeper than I thought, and my healing is still a work in progress. But I can say proudly that I committed to re-learning what free time felt like, getting back in touch with the creative side of my personality, and refusing to jump every time my phone buzzed.

What happened next, I couldn't have dreamed, let alone planned.

Like a magnet, the real me began attracting some of the most *amazing* opportunities. Job offers began falling into my lap when old clients found out that I was on my own; they told their colleagues about my business acumen and unique operations skill set kicked up with a creative twist. Within six weeks of leaving my old job, I had a full client roster and a waitlist.

These clients didn't want me because I was a Yes Woman. They wanted me because I was smart, quirky, and brutally honest.

They wanted me because I was *me.*

And Mike? Despite his lack of a conclusive diagnosis, he began regaining mobility over time. He was back at work for half days in April of 2020, and full-time by June with 100 percent of his mobility back. Whether you call it a coincidence or a miracle, I call it a sign that my decision to start over brought everything back into alignment, both personally and professionally.

As women, we create life. Our gift is to be the fixers, the bridgers, the assuagers—and it feels natural for us to smooth the edges enough to make things comfortable for everyone else. But we must also learn that sometimes we have to let ourselves feel pain so that we're spurred into doing something about it.

The harsh reality is, not everything is worth holding on to. Sometimes the solution is to wipe the slate clean and start over, armed with the lessons that the experience taught us. In business, we call this the "sunk opportunity cost"—the idea that something is not worth keeping just because we've spent time or money on it.

It's never too late to admit that you're at your lowest, and do something about it. Hell, you may even start to like the dirt that gets under your fingernails on your climb back up to the top.

WALKING TOWARD MYSELF

CHRISTINE AMERMAN

PART OF ME—the loudest part—wanted to die. It couldn't see a future where I was happy and thriving, so it wished I was dead instead.

I felt done.

I'd done my best, hadn't I? And this is what I'd gotten: divorced at forty-one. My worst fears were confirmed. I was alone. And if I was alone, then who was I?

For the last four decades, I'd striven and pushed and burned out to take care of everyone else in the hopes that it would make me happy. Because that was what it meant to be a good person, right?

A good girl.

A good Christian.

A good wife.

A good mother.

Every day of my existence had gone toward making myself the person I thought I should be—the person others expected me to be. In middle school, I'd written letters to my future husband, quoting Mariah Carey lyrics and pouring out my hopes and dreams for our perfect life together. I put them in my kid-sized safe with reverence and every intention of giving them to him one day. As a high schooler, I was firmly self-ensconced in purity culture, raptly note-taking at Josh Harris' (of *I Kissed Dating Goodbye* fame) live events.

I proudly wore a self-chosen purity ring and saved my virginity until my wedding night. I truly believed that if I followed all the rules, my reward would be a happy marriage, a wildly fulfilling sex life, and the realization of all my dreams. Every vision of my future included a man beside me, and I longed for the romance and adventure I found in books. I was in love with the fairy tale, with the belief that another human would make me whole and fill me up—would be my prince, as cheesy as it sounds. For my high school graduation, my parents gave me a beautiful print of the scene in *Cinderella* where she and the prince are married, and they even took me to dine at the Magic Kingdom's Cinderella Castle. I was *that* dedicated to this idea for my own life.

In college, I dreamed of starting my own company with my best friends and boyfriend. I dreamed of the freedom to run the show, travel, choose who I worked with, have total control of my income, and be fulfilled by the work I was doing. We talked about it, but that was where the action stopped—and stayed dormant for years. I convinced myself it was because I didn't have a clear plan, but in truth, it was because I didn't trust myself to figure it out. I was terrified, and ultimately, it wasn't what I believed I was "supposed" to do.

I would tell my boyfriend—my first love, the one I thought would be forever—that my worst fear was being abandoned or cheated on because that would mean that all the work I'd put in, giving everything I had with every fiber of my being, wasn't enough. That *I* wasn't enough. With him, I was determined to make a perfect ending happen—that's what you did when you found love, right? And they all lived happily ever after? Despite multiple break-ups, red flags, and his unwillingness to commit, I kept trying. All along, I was thinking, *I'm the problem if this won't work.*

After I finally ended things for good (and he didn't finish the rom-com script by waking up, realizing he loved me, and winning me back in spectacular style), I worked on myself for a while, gaining some sense of security and agency in my own singleness. Of course, that's when multiple guys came out of the woodwork with interest in me, including a couple through eHarmony, where my sister had signed me up one night. She'd sat me down at our borrowed kitchen table, declared that all I did was work, and how was I ever going to meet someone that way? She poured me a glass of wine and read the personality assessment questions out loud, entering my answers and eventually paying for my first month on the site.

It was there that I connected with a man with whom I shared a close mutual friend—our friend used to be my roommate and this man had even slept in my bed while I was out of town, but our paths hadn't yet crossed until the time was right. The connection was there, love ensued, and thirteen months after meeting, we married in a beautiful ceremony. I wore my dream dress, and we were surrounded by family, close friends, and lots of love.

Our relationship was strained from the start by my unrealistic fairy-tale expectations, lack of experience with communication and conflict, and infertility. I experienced three early miscarriages, followed by a textbook-perfect pregnancy that unexpectedly ended in the full-term stillbirth of our daughter, Maeve Evalyn. The tragic loss of Maeve was followed by two pregnancies stressed by PTSD, but ultimately, we were proud to welcome Fiora and Aewyn, healthy and thriving, to our family.

From the outside, things looked picture perfect. I had the big house, the supportive partner, the beautiful children, the dogs, and an impactful, successful business. But under the surface ran the current of the pressure I put on myself to be perfect at the roles I found myself playing, to the exclusion of prioritizing my own self and happiness.

Ultimately, I abandoned myself in search of the fairy tale. I abdicated my own needs and desires again and again. At some point, even knowing what I wanted—as opposed to what I thought I should want—became elusive. I didn't speak my mind, set any boundaries, or take charge of my life or the consequences of it in any way.

Of course, though I knew about it deep down, I couldn't admit that I was aware of any of this at the time. I ignored that soft tug on my heart, hoping that doing all of the "right" things would somehow solve the underlying problem. Because, you know, that always turns out well.

I threw everything I had into my career because it was the only place I felt competent. I built a business called Life with Passion that counseled people to grow their own personal-brand businesses.

I loved this work, loved helping other people find their authentic voice, loyal audience, and dream clients. I dreamt of traveling the world, inspiring people from big stages, creating massive global impact and an income to go along with it. My entire identity and worth were taken over by work—if I wasn't successful at this, I told myself, I had nothing. I *was* nothing.

No pressure, right?

As you might imagine, the illusion unraveled in spectacular fashion. My body rebelled, my adrenals going into overdrive and spiking, creating extreme anxiety. I was overwhelmed by the stress and intensity of parenting and working and trying to be everything for everyone. I compounded the stress by judging myself for feeling this way. I numbed out in the evenings, desperate to create a relief valve for the self-imposed pressure cooker of my life. Within a couple of years, my body was so overworked that I flatlined, catapulting into a well of despair and lack of motivation that had me uncontrollably crying under a tree in my backyard for hours each day. I was terrified that I was dying and would never again feel like myself. I wished for an end, an escape, relief from this overwhelm.

Unrealistic expectations, people pleasing, codependency, toxic emotions, and all the roles I'd taken on in order to be "good," combined to produce a sludge that mired me. I felt truly trapped, like my existence was not worth it. But I had these two little souls to care for who kept telling me they really wanted me here on Earth with them. So, I stayed. I thought it was the only option.

I continued to walk on eggshells.

I cycled through fight, flight, freeze, fawn, and flock.

I processed the trauma with loving friends for *years*.

89

I used my high-achieving persistence to try to become the person who could make my husband happy—while expecting that he was doing the same for me.

This brought me to a place where I didn't even know how to be at home in my own life, didn't even know what I wanted anymore. I knew that trying to hold on to my fairy tale wasn't an option anymore; I needed to get out of this relationship. But I was frozen by fear—fear of being alone and discovering that I wasn't enough, fear of screwing it all up, fear of being selfish. I was terrified that I wouldn't be able to rebuild if I burned my life down. Mostly, though, I feared things over which I had no control.

How would my girls interpret this seismic shift in their previously "stable" life? How would I mess them up by making this decision? How would I even explain it to them?

How would my extended family interpret me being *the very first one* in our family to get divorced?

It came back to freedom, freedom of choice. If freedom is what I value most, then why was I not living it? Was I creating a future that I actually wanted to live in? Was I being present and making my second act of life better than my first?

I often think about the family member I most resemble, my grandmother, Althea. She lived in a time when women had far fewer options. She gave up everything—including a fellowship at Harvard in the 1940s!—to fulfill the expected role of a woman when she fell in love. She went on to suffer through trauma and disillusionment when that relationship didn't fulfill her dreams, and died young because there weren't resources or outlets for her to properly heal and thrive in her own second act.

Choosing myself is not certain, but then, nothing ever really is. In the words of my three-year-old daughter, "I was scared, and then I was brave." So, I finally said the most difficult, bravest words of my whole life:

"I think we should split up."

The following several months were the biggest roller coaster of my life, full of the most profound and tangled grief, excitement, anxiety, depression, overwhelm, and fear I've ever experienced— and that includes the months following the loss of my daughter. (I thought I'd already established a rock bottom at that point; I was wrong.) I moved in with my parents and started spending half my time alone, figuring out myself. The other half of the time, I was learning how to solo parent my wonderfully and exhaustingly energetic and enthusiastic youngsters.

I was confronted with the dichotomy of living exactly the way I knew to be best for all of us, on one level, and feeling—surprisingly to me—profoundly terrified on a deeper level because all of my "security" and "shoulds" had been stripped away. The practices of surrender and trust became daily, often minute-by-minute, invitations to acceptance as I worked (and still work) with training my nervous system and DNA to accept and integrate the seismic shifts I've created.

This is the great experiment of my life, and it is a literal trust fall into the unknown.

My desperate attempts to be the person I was expected to be, to have the perfect job and nuclear family, and to cling to the security of some fairytale ending, have brought me here. To this place of surrender and trust in each moment where I am alone —and that is my power. I alone have the power to choose what's best for me. Even better, I know that when I choose me, everyone in my life benefits. Am I walking toward myself, toward the true version of me? Or am I walking toward a fantasy that will evaporate just like a mirage?

Life is for me, and I must be the one to live it.

10

PHOENIX FROM THE ASHES

JENN EDDEN

I **ALWAYS SAY** I was *so* stubborn that, for God to get my attention about his plan for me and my life, he had to literally blow up my house. And by that, I mean my husband Joe and I are survivors of a near-death gas explosion.

Just four months married, we arrived at our house late in the evening on January 23, 2003. I had just flown home from a work event and was tired, ready to take a shower and go to sleep. I got out of the car and could see my breath—it was that cold. Then, the thick scent of gas hit me.

Joe looked at me and said, "Jenn, we can't go in there. You can smell the gas from outside the house."

I said—because Lord knows I don't listen now and I for sure didn't listen back then—"Oh, I'm going in there. Ellie and Big Louie are in there and we need to get them out before this thing blows."

We quickly went into the house, calling our cats, hoping they would come out of hiding so we could get them to safety. I opened windows to try to air out the place, not realizing that it made the temperature inside decrease, and we were minutes away from the pilot light flicking on in the basement.

Joe called me several times asking me to get out of the house. Per usual, I didn't listen. I was too focused upstairs trying to find the cats. By now my heart was racing, and I could feel in my bones something bad was going to happen. I went back downstairs and stood in the back doorway, using my foot to hold open the thick wooden door while I called for the cats one more time. Suddenly, I saw a flash of light come from the basement doorway. I heard the loudest sound. It shook my body from head to toe. Essentially, the house had filled with gas and was one huge bomb.

When the pilot light went on ... *BOOM*.

The wooden back door splintered into a million pieces, and by the grace of God it didn't damage my eyes or break any bones in my face. In fact, the wooden shards missed my left eye by mere millimeters.

The funny thing is, when you survive a near-death experience, your mind shuts down long enough to forget the terrifying parts, so I have no memory between the sound of the explosion and me lying on the ground ten feet away. I didn't even know where I was. After getting me up and walking me over to our Jeep, Joe handed me some Dunkin' Donuts napkins from the glove box and explicitly told me not to look in the mirror, just keep pressure on my face.

At this point, what was left of the house was going up in flames. I was whisked away to the hospital, not knowing the state of our beloved pets, the damage to my face or our house. But we were alive.

The next morning, we returned to the house to see what the firefighters were able to salvage. Big Louie was curled up peacefully on the front lawn, his body cold, his eyes closed. We're not sure what happened, but he didn't make it. Ellie, on the other hand, was nowhere to be found, but I could sense she was still alive. I began calling her name with whatever voice I had left and heard the tiniest cry from the upstairs bedroom. Well, that was all I needed. We tore open the barricaded back door, ran upstairs, and there was Ellie, alive in my closet bedroom with only a few racing stripes of burnt fur. The running joke is that my huge collection of pocketbooks and shoes held back the fire long enough for Ellie to live!

After that almost fatal night, I was left with thirty-five stitches above and below my left eye, but I was grateful God spared my life. We lost everything except for Ellie, our Jeep Wrangler, our wedding photo album, and our wedding china. Somehow the photo album was beautifully preserved under all the rubble, and somehow the china didn't shatter when the firefighters chucked the unopened boxes out the open wall of what used to be our dining room. (Go figure. Great packaging on the part of Lenox!) But everything else—every bit of ephemera that made up our memories and represented our new life together—had burned to the ground.

There was a sense of unreality and chaos in the days and weeks after. We sifted through rubble—physically, emotionally, financially—and tried to find a way back to solid ground. But I wasn't a stranger to chaos. In fact, I'd spent much of my childhood in an unstable, explosive environment—though this one was emotionally explosive instead of literally. By this I mean there was always some kind of unpredictable chaos brewing or erupting in my family life. For example, the time our only car was supposedly stolen when Dad left it running to grab a candy bar at the convenience store. Sounds a bit fishy, right? Things simply never added up, and it left us constantly on uneven ground.

With that as my background, I wasn't exactly the most mentally stable of kids going through school. I woke up every day, frozen in bed, panicked about how I was going to make it through another day, month, or year. I felt anxiety about pretty much everything, to the point that it was unmanageable. I felt anxious about the bullying that I endured. I was stressed that I wasn't good enough, pretty enough, smart enough, cool enough. I was highly sensitive to the people and environments around me, which just magnified all the other feelings. I tried to put on a confident face, but everything felt out of control. And looking back, all of it stemmed from the unstable situation that was my home life.

Both of my parents spent much of my childhood dealing with undiagnosed or untreated mental illnesses. Though we appeared to the outside world as a "normal" family, problems slowly built up and eventually spiraled out of control—whether it was my dad getting himself into trouble with a dumbass business deal that almost lost us our house, or my mom sinking into a depressive episode and the bad days or weeks that would follow. My brother and I were always on high alert, waiting for the spinning plates to come crashing down. And when the plates inevitably fell, it always felt like it was up to us kids to pick up the pieces, even though we were ill-equipped to do so.

The worst of it was that we never talked about any of this as a family. It was just something that happened. If we couldn't find Mom, we'd ask Dad, and he'd say something like, "Oh, she's taking a break in the hospital." If we couldn't find Dad, the story was the same. It was never discussed or explained any further than that. I knew it wasn't something that happened to other people's parents, but in our house, that was the status quo, and we knew not to bring it up.

At the time I did not know that all the erratic behavior was part of an addictive pattern. It eventually became blatantly obvious that my dad was plagued by many addictions, the most obvious being his sex, lying, and sugar addictions. Couple that with him being diagnosed with bipolar disorder and depression, my mom's ongoing depression, and the multiple trips in and out of the psychiatric ward for both my parents, and our family was a breeding ground for raising kids with all sorts of addiction issues of our own.

My addiction of choice was sugar. I remember regularly coming home from school and eating two rows of Oreos like it was nothing. Or other nights, after track practice, I'd be so stressed out and hungry that I'd eat almost a half-gallon of ice cream. Turkey Hill mint chocolate chip was my poison of choice. To me, these behaviors didn't seem disordered, and no one in my family ever said anything about it. Back then I never stopped to think about why I was so addicted to sweet treats; they comforted me—at least momentarily—and that was good enough. But I've realized that, at least in part, I was missing sweetness, ease, and relaxation in my life, and I tried to fill the void with sugar.

I remember my lightbulb moment, the realization that I no longer had to live with the pain I was experiencing from overeating and indulging in too much sugar. *I have the ability to be in control*, I told myself, *if only I can put all the pieces together*. I created a new routine to manage out-of-control eating, and stuck to it, and it changed my life.

In the days that followed my house blowing up, I thought a lot about how God spared me. Of course, I wished the explosion hadn't happened at all, but sometimes we don't get to choose our path in life. Sometimes we think we're going one way, but there's an unavoidable detour that takes us in a completely different direction. In my case, this detour was one hell of a wake-up call that made me realize there had to be more for me to do with my life. After all, I was only twenty-eight!

But when you lose everything you own, the world kind of goes quiet. And in those moments, you can hear your own voice—really hear it.

I made a pact with God that I was going to find my mission. I call it my God moment. Having helped myself out of a deep, dark disorder, I knew I wanted to help others in a similar fashion. But I just hadn't found my way into that work despite going to osteopathic school to be a pediatrician and working for a nonprofit. Nothing stuck. I still felt a pull though, and before the explosion I often thought about how my experience growing up with parents who struggled with mental illness and addiction—and then struggling with those things myself—gave me a unique insight to help others in similar situations.

Within two weeks of my house blowing up, I applied to ten holistic, health-related schools around the country to see what piqued my interest. The focuses were different, from acupuncture to Ayurveda to nutrition, but basically, I was looking for anything alternative that didn't involve allopathic medicine. I gathered all the brochures that came in the mail, and one, for the Institute for Integrative Nutrition, struck me at a soul level. I called Joe at work and said, "This is it, I found it. I am going to be a certified holistic health counselor. This is what I'm going to do with my life: I am going to help other women feel better."

Twenty years later, I am the founder of the Sugar Freedom Method, and CEO of a woman-led company helping busy female professionals who desire to break their own cycles of sugar addiction but lack the time, tools, and know-how.

I often find myself taking a deep breath and stepping back to allow in all I've accomplished in my personal and professional life. Old tendencies toward anxiety loom in the background—always, but the difference now is that I can see beyond what's causing them. It helps that my twenty-year marriage is built on a rock-solid foundation of trust, mutual respect, joy, and high levels of communication. With all that said, are there still days where I eat sugar? Absolutely! But the big difference is that it's under my control now. I can have a treat without the guilt, shame, or bingeing.

I truly believe with every ounce of my being that our past does not need to define us nor predict our future; just because we were born into a family with addiction and emotional upheaval, doesn't mean that as adults we can't create our own security and our own freedom from addiction. We all have the opportunity to think whatever the hell we want and to be whoever the hell we came here to be!

I know that if you want something badly enough, it is yours for the taking. More importantly, you are loved enough and deserve to have it.

For me, life is a gift every day—the present is the real present. The day I decided to make my family's mess my mission was the day that my light got a little brighter. I knew that no setbacks, no matter how explosive they might be, would ever take me down for good. Sometimes, "burning it all down" is what it takes to rebuild with an unshakable foundation.

Healing will never be a straight line; it's a journey with ups and downs, and those setbacks or detours are only temporary. You'll come out the other side stronger and wiser.

And what fun would life be without a few detours, anyway?

THE PLANS I HAVE FOR YOU

DIANE CAINE

I CALL HIM and he picks up. "Hey, what's up?"

"Are you on the way? The girls are wondering when Daddy is coming to meet us."

"Yeah, yeah, I can't talk right now. I'm still on the field."

"Okay, well, call me when you're coming." He agrees hastily and hangs up.

Interesting. He doesn't ever take his cell phone onto the softball field. And anyway, I know that's not where he's at—because I'm in my car, parked in the emergency room parking lot, perfectly positioned to see the door, waiting.

And there he is, pulling his truck into the lot, right on time. He is on the phone having a little chat, and it's not with me. The ER door swings open and she emerges, still on her phone. She saunters over to his truck and they both hang up. He hands an iced coffee out the window to her. She proceeds to get into the passenger side.

I'm watching, blood boiling. Trying to breathe. She nestles right into his shoulder and he wraps his arm around her, kissing her forehead.

Now I've seen enough.

I get out of my car and start to walk over. He finally sees me when I'm about three feet away. I can hear him utter, "Oh, shit!" through the open window. He's trying to move away, but she's not cooperating; instead, she's watching me with a little Cheshire Cat grin on her face.

***

I met my husband, whom I'll call Steve, just nine months after losing my fiancé, Glenn, in a fatal car accident. When I first met him, I thought he was cute and we flirted. However, I wasn't really interested. I thought he was younger than me as he was hanging out at the fire station with my baby brother. I'm from a family of volunteer firefighters, and life revolved around the station—my place of comfort and safety as I grieved. It was where I could cry or hang out after work when I didn't know what to do with myself. I could numb my pain with alcohol, and they would make sure I got home safely.

At the annual Firefighter's Field Day, Steve asked me on a date. I told him I wasn't interested in dating someone younger than me. He asked me how old I thought he was.

"You're eighteen." I was twenty-one.

"Nope, I'm twenty-two," he said.

"Bullshit! You're hanging around, playing grab-ass with all the eighteen- and nineteen-year-olds."

"Do you want to see my license? I'll prove it to you."

He pulled out his license; sure enough, he was telling the truth.

I decided a date would be okay, though I wasn't ready for anything serious. I was still learning how to live all over again after losing Glenn. I was traveling to Connecticut every weekend to see his family and visit his grave. People were urging me to move on—I had my whole life ahead of me, they said, just not the one I had planned before the car accident. I knew I wanted to move on, eventually; I wanted to be married and have children, eventually.

Steve knew exactly what I had been through. He had been warned by my brother and everyone at the station. He was also put on notice: if he hurt me, he would answer to them. He was undeterred by any of it. When I told him I needed space, he gave it to me, but he was persistent, charming, and supportive.

A year later he proposed in grand fashion in the middle of the softball field during the annual fire department fundraising game. Roses, a huge sign, down on one knee, literally in the middle of the game. I said yes! We had a two-year engagement during which we moved in together and started planning our life.

We got married. We had two beautiful girls. We bought a house. He started his career as a firefighter, while I was building a successful business career. I got what I wanted: I was married, and I had babies I adored. He got what he wanted: his dream career and a woman his parents approved of. It *looked* like the perfect life playing out according to our perfect plan.

It wasn't.

I suffered with postpartum depression after the births of both girls. I was struggling with the guilt of having a career and wanting to be at home with the girls. I tried making the kids my full-time job for a while, only to discover I'm not really designed to be a stay-at-home mother. This only compounded the guilt.

Meanwhile, he was never home, either at the station or playing softball. Married life, it turns out, interfered with the life he really wanted: a life of freedom, with no obligations. He blamed me for his unhappiness. It didn't matter what I did: everything was my fault, nothing was enough. *I* was never enough.

At the time, I believed that no matter how difficult things got in our marriage, I'd made a vow—for better or for worse. I believed we could get through anything because we committed to each other. But we didn't want the same things.

Signs were everywhere, yet I wasn't ready to face them. He had lots of friends—all of whom I'd met, except for her. Six-hundred-dollar phone bills (back when we got charged by the minute for calls). Consistent late runs at the station. A hospital ID in his wallet that had her picture on it. I called the number on the phone bill, but she said they were simply friends. He said the same, kept telling me I had nothing to be concerned about, that I should take a chill pill. I tried to believe him, but there was always this nagging feeling in my gut.

Then, he started involving my daughters in his deceptions, and telling them to lie to me. One day when I returned home from work, the girls were so excited to tell me about their day, and then my youngest slipped and told the truth about who they had been with.

My oldest looked at her with horror in her eyes, "Shh! You weren't supposed to tell Mommy."

I lost it, cornering Steve in the living room with what I'd found out. But he kept gaslighting me, telling me they were just friends.

I couldn't tell him who to be friends with. I had nothing to worry about. Just *calm down.*

I knew I had decisions to make. What were my girls learning? What did I want them to see? Did I want them to see that it was perfectly okay for a married man to have a "friend" like that, and that I didn't value myself enough to stand up against it? Yet, I was still in denial. I needed proof that I wasn't losing my mind, that they weren't "just friends." I needed to see it for myself.

In the parking lot that day, I got my wish. I confronted them both and told him to come home, pack his shit, and get out. He never even opened the door of the truck. He didn't come after me as I stormed back to my car. He'd already made his choice.

Driving home, I shook like a leaf. I sobbed, turning beet-red as I navigated the streets. Even though I had said, "For better or for worse," it didn't matter. I was devastated and relieved all at the same time. Devastated at the ending of my marriage, at the emotional and verbal abuse I'd put up with for so long, that my life was not turning out the way I had planned it, that my girls were going to live in a "broken home." But I was also relieved that they didn't have to lie anymore, and that I wasn't losing my mind. I knew the truth, and my gut had not been wrong.

It was now time to start the healing process. I was grieving, just as I'd been when Steve and I met all those years before. This was a different kind of grief, though; it scrambles your eggs to have to continually engage with a person who's gone but not dead. With actual death, no matter how difficult, it's final—you never see your loved one again, you have a ritual of ending, and then learn to live without their physical presence. Divorce with children means you are not only dealing with your own pain, but also helping the kids navigate theirs. You are facing a "ghost" on a consistent basis, one you'd rather not have around, who stirs up old memories and anger. The only ritual to the ending of a marriage is a court date with a judge. There is no funeral; there is no remembrance of the love that started the marriage. There is simply the hurt, the anger, and the constant reminders that it's over.

I was left with very little self-esteem. I hated that my girls cried and missed their dad. I hated the mess he'd created. I blamed him. I blamed her. I blamed myself.

But now, I had choices to make. I chose me and my girls when I decided that infidelity was a deal breaker. Now, I needed to take the next step. Was I going to spend the rest of my days playing the victim and being bitter? Or was I going to be the victor, remembering the love, celebrating the lessons, and becoming better?

I chose to be better. It wasn't easy work; there were so many wounds to be healed, beliefs to overcome and to forgive.

Forgive him, forgive her, forgive myself.

As a woman of faith, I truly believe everything happens *for* us, not *to* us. My guiding light through losing Glenn, then divorcing Steve, was this verse, Jeremiah 29:11: "I know the plans I have for you, plans to prosper you, not to harm you. Plans for a future and a hope."

I continued to pursue my corporate career, and was promoted into an executive role. I started dating again. As I moved forward, I was open to the possibility of "happily ever after." I intentionally wrote out all of the traits I desired in my ideal mate. Shortly after, in a completely unpredictable and unexpected way, he showed up.

When people ask me how we met, I laugh and say, "I married the boy next door."

Bobby Caine bought the house across the street from my parents right around the same time Steve and I got engaged. I remember him coming across the street to introduce himself, and thinking what a kind man he was. He volunteered at the fire station with Steve, my brother, and my father. He saw me hugely pregnant with my first child, and later, his two boys played with my two girls at birthday parties.

Though we hadn't seen each other in several years, we reconnected at my brother's house about a year after my divorce, and I learned he was going through the same thing. His marriage was ending for the same reason mine had. He was as devastated as I had been, and was navigating many of the same challenges with his two boys as I had with my two girls. After seven years of dating, we decided to blend our families in 2014. Blending an all-girl house with an all-boy house with four teenagers was quite the adventure!

Bobby is my keeper; he truly loves me unconditionally. Our relationship is a beautiful gift that I am grateful for every day.

I wish I could say I have eradicated every limiting belief that gripped me in the wake of my divorce, but that would not be true. New challenges are always right around the corner. We have no control over the things that happen to us, but we do have a choice about how we respond to them. We may be responsible *to* others in our life, but we are not responsible for their decisions, their feelings, or their actions. We are responsible *for* ourselves, and ourselves alone.

As Bobby often reminds me, we must have the dark to appreciate the light. The challenges that I've experienced have led me to where I am today—to the person I am today. Life is an occasion. And I'm choosing to rise to it.

Rise into

CONNECTION

12

THE DAY I WALKED AWAY

ASHLEY COOK

I SAT ON THE COLD, HARD BENCH, frozen with nerves.

Jade slid into the booth opposite from me and looked across the table with her large, brown eyes.

I had questions. I hoped she had answers. More than that, I hoped her answers would be kind and calm the fears brewing inside of me.

I soon learned that wouldn't be the case.

Jade was the leader of a group I belonged to at a megachurch in the Dallas/Fort Worth area. To become a church member, applicants are required to join a group that is comprised of people who have the same anatomy and are in similar life stages. Group members are expected to tell everything about their lives to the other group members.

Yes. *Everything.*

A couple of weeks prior, a member of our group, Leslie, had shared that she was doing something the church deemed unacceptable. I watched, stunned, as Jade threatened to launch the church's discipline process on her. I hadn't grown up with such a thing, and learning about it jarred me. From what I could piece together, this discipline process involved repeated personal meetings with church leadership. In these meetings, the leaders would present a path of repentance and reconciliation. If the person didn't eventually "turn from their ways," their formal membership status would be revoked.

As I sat there silently, a wildfire of anxiety sparked to life within me. I believed quite differently than the church on many things. I now feared that if I acted differently from what the church sanctioned, I would fall subject to this discipline process, too.

"What questions do you have?" Jade asked—as always, getting straight to the point.

I exhaled sharply. The knot in my stomach tightened. "So, I have some questions about what happened with Leslie. I know she was doing something that the church didn't approve of, but I was wondering about something else."

Jade stared back at me, unblinking.

"I was wondering … can church discipline be launched for just actions or also for beliefs?"

Without hesitation, Jade said, "Both."

Great. That was the answer I feared hearing most. Now I knew with certainty that my beliefs could get me kicked out of this church.

The silence started growing between us, so I stammered, "Okay, but, but ... what if the belief doesn't lead to an action?"

(I have no idea why I asked this. I panicked, okay?)

Jade flicked her eyes at the ceiling for a brief second before locking them back with mine. "Like what? Do you have an example?"

An example? She wanted an *example*? I quickly combed through all the ways that I believed differently than this church.

I believed women could be whatever God called them to be. *That feels a bit risky to share.*

I didn't have any issue whatsoever with my LGBTQIA+ friends. *Oh, not today.*

I didn't believe that a man was the "spiritual head of the household." *Sister, please.*

So, I chose the most benign example I could think of—the rapture.

I shuffled in my seat. "Well ... like, okay. So, I don't believe that the rapture is scriptural."

I thought that would be a safe zone. Surely, if I could give a small, more acceptable example, I'd hear, "Oh, that's okay. We make allowances for differences like that." Then maybe my fears would be calmed, and I could continue with the status quo.

Instead, Jade's big brown eyes grew into saucers. Apparently, the rapture wasn't a safe topic after all. I knew at that moment that I'd chosen wrong.

From then on, the gnawing fear I had of getting kicked out of the church grew.

Here's the thing. I grew up in the church. I cut my teeth on Christian conservatism. I was confirmed and baptized in the Lutheran Church

Missouri Synod. In case you're wondering, back in the 1990s, they weren't exactly known as a beacon of progressiveness and women's empowerment.

I spent my teenage years holding hands around flagpoles praying for my classmates and the world's salvation. I wore oversized Jesus shirts emblazoned with statements like, "Satan is ugly as sin." I went to church on Sunday mornings, Sunday evenings, and Wednesday nights. I signed purity pledges and visited Crisis Pregnancy Centers. I shredded *Harry Potter* books and prayed against the demonic Victoria's Secret TV program that was sure to be the downfall of small-town American morality.

By all definitions, I was a good, quiet, Christian girl.

But there was one thing I never understood: why women couldn't be senior pastors. In the most spiritually high time of my life, I wanted to grow up and serve God in the most meaningful of ways. I wanted to be a pastor. But I was told no.

If only that was the end of it.

At college, I met my best friend Justin, a brilliant, gorgeous man with the most generous of hearts and a deep love for the movie *Steel Magnolias*. Like me, he'd grown up in conservative Christianity. Like me, he also dated men. Our friendship showed me another crack in my religious upbringing—that perhaps being gay wasn't the abomination I was taught.

The more LGBTQIA+ friends I made, the more joy, happiness, and flourishing we all experienced. The crack was becoming a chasm.

Over the span of the next fifteen years, I moved around the country working for different Fortune 500 companies. I attended Southern Baptist as well as Christian and Missionary Alliance churches. I tried

Presbyterian, Methodist, and Anglican churches. I hopped back over to a Southern Baptist church, because apparently, I didn't get enough fire and brimstone the first time. I was a true denominational mutt.

In the midst of that, I temporarily ditched the corporate world to go to seminary. That blew the doors off other tightly-held beliefs I had—the death penalty, the rapture, you name it. I also discovered the scriptural evidence that backed my long-held belief of how anatomy does not dictate calling—that women could be whatever and whomever they felt called to be. Most importantly, it gave me the freedom to question God and question religion.

In my corporate career, I was told that my questions threatened male leaders. In college, a Catholic priest once told me that my questions were intimidating. In my twenties, I was deeply involved in a church and a woman leader told me about a particular injustice she experienced as a female. I talked to a pastor about it, and instead of hearing a satisfactory answer—or any explanation, really—I was assigned a book to read on biblical womanhood. (I did not.)

Throughout my life as a Christian, I teetered on the edge of rocking the boat and playing the game. Most of the time, I did the latter. I'd recalculate, shapeshift, and fall back in line. I'd walk on eggshells in the name of the Lord. I'd be a good Christian girl.

Over time, I learned how to ask questions and bring up concerns in non-threatening ways. I played this game in the cubicle and in the pew. I like to think I pulled it off quite well.

And yet, here I was again, poking the holy rollin' bear. I sat on that bench, asking Jade questions and facing that crossroads—play the game or rock the boat.

This time felt different though. More was at stake. This time, I might get kicked out of the church.

The thought of that was terrifying. I didn't want to jeopardize my sense of community, opportunities to volunteer, and a familiar place to worship and spiritually grow. I had much to lose.

See, I was knee-deep in this non-denominational megachurch. I was a leader in their anti-sex trafficking ministry. I was a faithful attendee on Sundays and often during the week. I was a member of a community group that met religiously (pun intended) and was expected to live like an open book, no matter how gross it got. And every week, I walked into that church with my beliefs shoved down in my pockets, too timid to let them see the light of day.

Unlike before, when I'd played the game and fallen in line, I knew that this time I couldn't keep silent. Witnessing this church launch a discipline process on a person who didn't conform to what they wanted triggered a fear in me based upon what I had experienced both in corporate America and in churches—conform, or be rejected.

Questions are okay ... as long as you don't ask too many of them.

I left lunch that day feeling let down. I knew that, if it came down to it and I ended up leaving this church, it wouldn't be like before. It wouldn't be quiet.

My community group and I met with leaders for a formal mediation. I let them know how highly toxic this was and that I could have no part in it. Apparently, others felt the same as I did, and our group dissolved.

I spoke to a few others in the church about what was going on. I talked to some trusted faith leaders from my past for their counsel. I combed through articles written by the head pastor and skimmed through his social feed.

The more I dug, the worse I felt.

Then, the pastor publicly posted some harsh statements about a particular group of marginalized people. These statements were unkind and not reflective of the God I knew.

The pastor's comments tipped the scales, and I knew at that moment I could no longer be part of that church. I typed out my resignation letter. It was my first time really taking a stand like this, and I wanted to be thoughtful and clear. I pored over every word and asked trusted mentors of mine read it for feedback. I tweaked and reworded and edited it over and over again.

Of all my experiences with that church, I was most nervous about sending this email. After I sent it, every time I peeped into my inbox, I could feel my throat closing and stomach fluttering. My body and mind were wracked with uncertainty and fear of what the response would be.

Eventually, one came.

My resignation was rejected.

Well, now what? I hadn't planned for that.

The leader wanted to talk about my letter and see if there was any way we could reconcile. While I sighed at the thought of not having closure, I appreciated her kind response. So, I replied and set up a time to chat by phone. She heard me out and tried to encourage me. After our conversation, she sent some more articles for me to read and put me in touch with another leader.

The thing was, by this point, there were no words to read or conversations to have that could squelch my conviction. I didn't need more information. I needed to be heard, and for what I said to matter.

I knew in my heart that church was no longer safe for me. It was time to leave. So, I sent over a newly minted resignation letter and officially left for different pastures.

Breaking up with a church can be agonizing. It's messy and hurtful and comes with a hefty dose of disillusionment. I wish I could say that I enthusiastically joined another church after that experience. I wish I could say that I got deeply involved with a new congregation and lived happily ever after in the name of Jesus. This isn't the case for me.

Church has become like a troubled ex. When things were good, they were *really* good. But there's also a reason you broke up, and it's not always a good idea to get back together—at least not right away. It takes time and healing. It takes unraveling what went sideways and getting back on solid ground, so you don't repeat mistakes. It takes distance to see things for what they really are, to learn more about who you are, what you believe, and how to be at peace with that.

But there's still a longing, right? Leaving a church is hard because your friends are there. You serve there. Sometimes, your family is there. Your social network, volunteer opportunities, and spiritual growth are all tied to the very place that is now causing you heartache and harm.

Just because you leave a church doesn't mean you leave the desire to be loved and accepted and welcomed just as you are. It also doesn't mean you're a backslider, wayward, or rebellious. It doesn't mean you've lost your faith or belief in God, though it can also mean that. And if you live in the South, breaking up with religion is not a condition upon which someone looks at you with dewy eyes, pats your arm, and says, "Bless your heart. Let me add you to my prayer chain."

I've come to learn that some spiritual spaces are safer than others. Sometimes, you find more grace outside the walls of the church than inside it. For the more daring, it means you find God beyond the systems, organizations, and institutions, and discover that God is right there with you in the dirt.

I'll take that over a stiff old pew any day.

I've also realized that I'm not alone in my story. The more I share this story and others like it, the more other women step forward and say, "This happened to me, too." I usually have a mixed response to those statements. I feel relieved I'm not alone, but sad this isn't an isolated event. It's not just me.

I've learned a lot since sitting on that cold, hard bench that day with Jade. I've untangled and let go of a lot. I used to be afraid to do such things. Now I know there's grace in the unraveling if we have the eyes to see it and the heart to lean into it.

That day with Jade was the first time I really stood up for myself—for something that meant the most to me: my faith. I remembered how important it is for all of us to unmute ourselves, to ask questions, and above all else, to tell our stories.

This time, I wasn't silent.

13

AT THE GATE OF HEAVEN

LISA ROCHE

YOU HAVE A GATHERING *of women behind you. Hundreds of ancient women standing there, arms outstretched, hands touching your shoulders. You are supported by them. Their heads are bowed in reverence and gentle genuflection for the role you are accepting.*

Your lineage is these women, natural Healers who never stepped into their gifts or refused them outright. Hundreds of women who were called to heal, but out of fear and persecution, refused and snuffed out their light. They are in awe. They are standing behind you, supporting and guiding you.

These ancient Healers will now work through you to deliver miraculous healing of spirit to whomever you work with. This is the gift they are delivering through you. Through you to all.

You, as a Healer, must share this with as many people as possible.

***

For years, I lived in deliberate rejection of the word "healer." I dismissed even the slightest hint of the role and title. I told myself I was just really good at my job.

I was a loving, caring, and talented Gyrotonic Instructor. For close to two decades, I had used the Gyrotonic Method to help people with their physical ailments, guiding them through the spiraling exercises to open their tissue and expand their spines to invite healing and peace into their bodies and minds. I had gained a reputation for being able to intuitively know exactly what a client needed to make a full recovery, and clients stayed with me for years because of that mysterious feeling of wonder that takes hold at every session.

But no, I'd insist, I was no Healer. It was enough to force myself to admit I was just really good at what I did. "Healer" was a word that stung my eyes and made my head spin, that struck at my stomach and made me lurch. A word that produced panic and terror in every cell of my body. "Healer" was a title reserved for the special few, the blessed, people who create miracles and are chosen by God—right? It was a word that made people magical and separate from others. A word that elevated its bearer, shone a light on them, and drew attention.

That wasn't me. Who was I to declare myself better than others—or, heaven forbid, special?

For my entire life, I had shackled myself to a lie, one I fully believed. It held me back, kept pushing my head underwater so it was all I could do to reach the surface and breathe. I was haunted by a repeated monologue summed up in one sentence:

You are not special.

I lived in those words. I embodied the concept of staying small, remaining hidden, head down, eyes forward, and quiet.

You are not special. I infused those words into the fiber of my being, the fabric of my soul, so deep that the very concept kept me comforted in a twisted, delusional way. *If I'm not special, no one sees me. If no one sees me, I can't be judged. If I can't be judged, I can't be told I'm wrong or less than.*

But I also felt that if no one could say I was wrong, then they couldn't prove me right either. They couldn't turn the spotlight on that whisper that constantly inundated my head: *You are not special.* If I could hide the whisper from everyone else, then perhaps it wasn't true.

Around and around, for close to fifty years, I lived in that circular argument, simultaneously running from and embracing the fear of not being special. I was constantly chasing the safety and solitude of mediocrity in hopes that I wouldn't be noticed.

The problem with running in a circle is you only ever run from yourself. And you only ever catch yourself, too.

That's where I found myself one spring day, in the familiar space of a lightworker, hearing those words about the gathering of women standing behind me. I had run full circle, away from and toward *myself.* Me, my soul, my truest self—the beginning and the end of a struggle and race I hadn't even realized I had been running.

In that room, surrounded by light purple walls and held by brilliant sunlight, I stared at an organized line of colorful spiritual books so as to not cry and dissolve into my fear. A picture of an angel rising into a burst of light hung on the wall, and it brought me particular comfort. Behind me was a massage bed, a solid structure in my auric field. And on that day, I was grateful for its presence, because in humbled awe, I crumbled onto it. That message was not what I had expected for my session. Who would ever anticipate that kind of immense blessing?

I felt my emotions pulling in opposite directions. I was crushed under the enormity of the responsibility that was laid out before me. Crushed under the humility of being chosen for such a blessing. Crushed by the generosity of my elders to teach, guide, and work through me. Crushed—and yet, I felt elated for all the same reasons. In a whirlwind of confusion and emotion, conflicting thoughts rushed through my brain. *If I accept the title of Healer, what will others think? If I call myself a Healer, what does that say about who I think I am? If I tell the world, what if I can't deliver?* I felt an overwhelming need to kneel on the ground and lower my head to the floor. An eternity passed in minutes, and I vacillated between the feelings of not being worthy and humbled grace. I wallowed in the inner turmoil that every person faces as they stand at the entrance of their own gates to heaven. *What if I walk through?*

But in the safety of this healing space, a light shined into the darkest of shadows to force me to genuflect in reverence to my own worth. I dropped to my knees and released my internal struggle with worthiness, ego, and fear. With shallow breath, I sat and cried as decades of confusion and grief flowed out of me. Then, layer by layer, my soul tore away at the doubt—*You are special*, it told me. *You have always been special.* Feeling the strength of the souls who had gathered to anoint me, I finally settled. With the entirety of my being, I accepted my role as Healer.

It was most definitely a conscious effort to accept this role. It took strength, fortitude, and faith to step into this ascended title. On shaking legs, I rose off the floor. Through closed eyes, I could sense the enormous gateway before me, the entrance into a new existence. All of my senses lit up as I took in the momentousness of what stood before me. I felt a spark of strength and covered my eyes with my hands, an involuntary act of humility and grace. Standing before my own personal portal, I said yes and stepped through.

Emboldened with purpose and supported by a power I had never before experienced, I took a deep breath and lowered my hands from my eyes, allowing the tears to stream down my face. In perfect timing, light shone through the window, and I felt the warmth of divine love drench over me in a holy ritual. I accepted the title of Healer and felt a crown placed upon my head.

Immediately, I was filled with the gratitude of every woman in my lineage—every Healer who was ever denied or forced to retreat from their natural abilities. Out of our collective fear, I was healed. And then, birthed anew from their courage, I stepped into my new role and somehow intuited the contract I was enacting. This contract was written at the creation of my soul, but in that moment of affirmation, it activated. I think of it as a soul contract of love and servitude to help others heal and find their way back to their soul's purpose. It was as if I had been stumbling around in darkness, but when my hand closed on the gate, I threw it open to reveal an eternity drenched in sunlight. There is deep solitude and peace in knowing and embracing your soul's purpose. I walked through the gate and found myself defined, whole and worthy of divine understanding and direction.

My guides were kind, gentle, and patient as I learned how to raise my vibration and open myself to their knowledge. Almost immediately, my sessions with clients were altered completely. With the acceptance of faith, my fear of being seen and valued was obliterated. My doubt was erased; there was no room within me for negative emotions or worries. I was shown in each moment that every question had an answer and, if I allowed for it, guidance would lead me to serve someone in the best way possible. There was not a trace of self-doubt left as I leaned into the support of my ancient Healers.

With their example and expertise, my confidence grew as I was shown exactly how physical pain and disease are birthed from the energy of trauma. They taught me that emotional pain is the seed from which the plant of fear roots and grows. Fear then metastasizes, growing into the manifestation of diseases and ailments that deteriorate the human form. Client after client, I was shown how to find and release the energy of fear and trauma to alleviate future ailment.

Every day, I share in the energy of miracles and help others to release their fear so that they may find themselves at the entrance of their own gate and have the courage to walk through.

This is my life, a never-ending learning experience, and I love it. I am no longer wandering in a state of self-doubt, living in fear of being discovered. I'm not hiding from my true self or wearing masks to be accepted. I speak my truth, express my needs, and am empowered by my authenticity. My relationships are supportive and nurturing because I speak with clarity. My life is in alignment with my soul's purpose, and every day is filled with adventure, peace, and growth. I couldn't be more grateful or in more awe for how much I have changed. I am proud of who I am and how I live in service not just to others, but to myself and to a life that is in complete celebration of me.

So, I ask you: Why have you come here? Why are you reading this? Are you ready to walk through your doubt, release your fear, and heal your trauma so that you too may discover your soul's purpose? Are you ready to embrace yourself? And I mean fully, wholly, the light and the shadow—are you ready to embrace your truest self?

Who are you? What is your purpose? What makes you special? Share yourself with the world, as I have shared myself with you.

I am Lisa: wife, mother, daughter, sister, friend, and Healer.

14

BET ON YOU

PORTIA MICHELE

PALMDALE, CALIFORNIA, 2021. My little black Kia Soul is parked on the side of the Route 14 freeway. I'm a thirty-year-old, anxiety-ridden, enraged, and yet eerily calm Black woman.

The sweet woman on the other end of the "number you dial when you try to kill yourself due to work-related instances" is calmly asking me how I got here. How did I get to the point of wanting to run my car off the road, and still somehow manage to have a portion of my psyche intact enough to call the helpline?

How in the fuck did losing a job I hated take me to the point of being ready to end it all?

I settled. That's how.

At that point in my life, I had all the things I thought I wanted, but they had all gone terribly wrong. A turning point. For five years, I climbed my way up the corporate ladder, achieving my "dream job," only to have it come crashing down when it turned out not to be anything I thought it would be. I developed crippling anxiety, my entire body was in pain, and I was vomiting daily. My doctors thought I had cancer.

I began seeing a therapist for the first time and was introduced to the concept that I was actually a human being, not a robot, and could not keep up the sixty-five-plus-hour workweeks expected of me. My therapist showed me that my symptoms pointed to stress. It wasn't cancer. I took a medical leave to rejuvenate so I could go back to my dream job.

Unable to hack the pressure of it all, I buckled, and ended up in a lower position at half the pay and with no way to supplement enough income to afford the San Diego, California lifestyle that my wife and I had previously enjoyed. We moved back in with my parents, and our cracked relationship shattered. To top it all off, I was cut off from my community where I sourced my inspiration. I couldn't coach. I was at my wits' end.

I was shocked to feel so full of rage. I hated my job at this point—so, wasn't this freedom what I wanted? Why was I so angry?

Well, I was angry because I had sold myself out, and I knew it.

You see, my marriage, my career accomplishments, my status in my community, were the ways I showed myself I was worthy of anything. I was good because I was a loyal wife. I was special because I was the boss everyone wanted to have. I was loved because the people in my life couldn't imagine their life without me in it.

Without those ways of measuring my worth, I was nothing and no one.

I'm sure I don't need to tell you that career, status, and other people's expectations ain't exactly a formula for happiness—and that's what the woman on the other end of the line said. Then, she called my next of kin, making arrangements to ensure I wouldn't harm myself or others as I went about the business of figuring out what to do with this nothingness.

The beauty of the bottom is that *any* option seems better than the ones you are presented with. After realizing my worth was tied up in all the wrong things, I was left with a gap. I asked myself, *What can I attach my worth to if my job isn't who I am? Who am I?*

How would I determine my identity without the external validation I had come to believe was necessary to breathe air, to exist?

In that time of uncertainty, I looked to that all-too-familiar millennial balm, YouTube, and decided to figure out three things:

Thing 1: What does it mean to be a soul in a body? I had heard the phrase a hundred times, but that hadn't brought me any closer to understanding what it meant. By that point, I was well versed in the New-Age personal development world, having been introduced to a rigorous Tony Robbins-like curriculum in my early twenties. As effective as that had been to get me unstuck before, it left me with empty hands during this current turn of events. It wasn't gonna help me find my soul.

Thing 2: What in the world was special about me? Up until this point, I was aware that I was loved, I knew how to be good at my job, and once people got to know me, they seemed to like me. But in all honesty, I couldn't understand why. What was it about me that really made a difference for people? There had to be something, and I was determined to discover it for myself.

Thing 3: What the hell was I going to do now? What did I really want out of life, now that life had hit the restart button on my behalf? I knew I had something to offer—but what it was, how I could work it, and what I was going to do about it? I had no clue.

So, I searched. For months, I dove into all things metaphysical: mythologies, ancient religions, magic, tarot, star seeds, astrology, crystals, herbs, mediumship, and witchcraft—right alongside soap making, candle making, jewelry construction, metal work, wood burning, floral arranging, and whatever else sparked my interest.

I realized that it was the first time since childhood that I had time on my hands, so I just let myself play in the YouTube sandbox. All the while, I was discovering myself again, allowing myself the time and energy to have interests—to be inspired for inspiration's sake without the expectation of an output, and without the gaze of needing to produce something.

It woke me the fuck up.

Suddenly, I was leaping out of bed in the morning, telling everyone in my house about my new discoveries. Making crystal-infused body butters, necklaces, and candles for family and friends. Running everyone's charts, pulling their cards, and having long, late-night chats about feelings, and the stars, and their beliefs, and how they rationalized their pain. It unlocked hidden abilities I didn't even know I had. I had found a piece of my joy. The Universe, God, the power that be, whatever you want to call it, responded quickly.

I had a real affinity for the spiritual stuff. I now recognize that inner knowing and speedy acumen to be supported by my guides and ancestors. Of all the modalities that I dove into, African Spiritual Traditions, specifically hoodoo and ancestral veneration, were the most influential. As soon as I began a relationship with the energies of my ancestors, it was like rocket fuel poured on anything I set my mind to. A lot of people call this "manifesting."

I didn't really have words for it at the time, but I was "manifesting" like a motherfucker. I would say to someone, "Man, I wish I could have this experience"—and *bam*, there it would be.

I wanted to go to the Smart Funny & Black concert with Amanda Seales, featuring Dwayne and Whitley from the show *A Different World*, but there was no way I could come up with the money for tickets, and the show sold out in days. Like magic, a friend called to tell me that, not only did she have tickets, but I could go for free.

I casually mentioned that maybe I would like to sell the candles and body products I was making, not truly believing I could. People spent years perfecting their formulas, scent throws, and fragrance-to-wax ratio; how could I do something so complicated with so little experience? *Boom!* Almost instantly, the formulas, business plan, and marketing strategy started popping into my head, like I was a computer downloading software there was no way I should've had access to.

I felt like the lady in the *Fifth Element*; I would go to sleep and wake up with vast amounts of knowledge. What I was learning certainly wasn't on YouTube.

Clients started flowing in, seemingly without me trying. And, all of a sudden, I had a business.

Let me take this moment to inform or remind you: as a fat, Black, queer woman in this world, there are few advantages I have over the default society in which I live. Being of a lineage that has survived the unforgivable, been persecuted, underfunded, under-resourced, let down, purposefully led astray, and still managed to create a generation of thriving human beings ... well, let me just say that I have an army of some of the most well-resourced ancestors to have ever existed. This is my advantage.

Once I slowed down enough to listen to their wisdom, and got still and quiet enough to hear the small voice of my intuition, nothing was ever the same. This was my work to do.

Did I learn how to navigate the business space as an entrepreneur? Yes. But the *real* work was learning to understand how I accessed myself, my soul, and my spiritual team—which in turn led to my joy, my dreams, my clarity of vision, and my discernment.

Things moved fast after that. Within a year, I had a full-blown spiritual product business. Within two years, I was coaching other business owners professionally. That thing I had been doing for free for almost a decade as my "god work" now had structure, methodology, and was paying my bills full-time.

Today, I'm living a soul-aligned, mission-driven reality. And *man*, am I making an impact! As of this writing, I've coached well over 300 clients, and had the ability to hold them through the darkest of nights, a global pandemic, and racial uprising. Through sudden deaths, ever changing political landscapes, insurmountable business shifts, and more. I've been blessed to support businesses to make their way over the seven-figure line, mentored some of the most brilliant humans on Earth to excavate their own genius, and watched them literally change the planet before my eyes. I have empowered countless healers like myself in their ability to live off of their magic, to give to the world in a way that is sustainable and defies the financial norms of their industries. I live in accordance with a life I really, really fuck with. This is my dream fulfilled.

Along the way, I've learned some big lessons. And, being a coach, I'm going to share them with you.

First, take time for *you.* You are worth it. You are a human: a brilliant wonder of magic wrapped in skin. Because you breathe and are living, you are deserving of joy. You deserve a life you fuck with, and it is your sacred mission to relentlessly pursue that life. Period. As long as you are not harming yourself or others, let no one deter you from the mission.

Next, don't spend your life living someone else's design. Discover yours. Make time to discover your own rules. See yourself as an adventure, constantly evolving and worth journeying to, over and over again.

And finally, trust the redirections. If life isn't going the way you planned, stop to consider that the plan might have been shitty. No shade, but was that plan *really* for the highest and greatest good?

As I've shared, pretty much everything in my life went wrong at one time. But everything in my life at that point was there because I thought it was *supposed* to be there, not because it was my dream. I had been running so hard after what I thought I wanted, I never stopped to check in and dream a new dream.

Folks love to say, "Live your dream, never stop betting on yourself," but let's face it: some of us never *started* betting on ourselves. We don't exactly live in a world that shows us it is safe to dream up a life we truly want. That only happens in movies, right?

Wrong, you can have it too.

Have a dream. Slow down long enough to dream it. Discover your joy, unlock your brilliance, and let the Universe lay a path for you to achieve your destiny.

And then, never give up.

Mark my words, you'll look up five years later and find yourself living a dream bigger than your old self could ever conjure. I've only just started, and I'm too young to be writing as if I have all the lessons figured out—but this one, I'm sure of. It's called Bet on You, and you can take it to the bank every time.

I know I did.

15

LOVE IS ENOUGH

LINDA LINDQUIST

THE MIDDAY SUN on the Baja peninsula felt like the blast of an oven as Ken and I watched a precious little boy walk away from us to rejoin his barefoot friends circling up for a game with a stick and a ball. At first, Ken had refused to show me the photo he had taken. Now, with wide eyes and a shaking hand, he handed over the fully developed picture. It showed Lisa and me smiling with our arms around our little friend, who beamed from ear to ear, proudly holding a blue plastic cup.

As I looked more closely, my heart froze, and I gasped. My soul sensed evil, and my knees buckled.

***

Seven months earlier ...

Fidgeting on a collapsible seat in the Francis Parker auditorium, where every Sunday a myriad of young, single, urban professionals gathered for church, I stared at the weekly bulletin screaming out the announcement of Abby Jill's upcoming mission trip to Mexico. In December I'd promised myself and Abby Jill that, if the international sailing project I was leading was canceled, I'd give myself the gift of going with her in May. Time now on my hands, I wrote my check, went to the pre-trip meeting where I met my fellow sojourners, and received our assignment. "Choose a verse that feels relevant to you for this trip." To this day, I do not know how I chose John 4:18–19, but it has been my life mantra ever since:

There is no fear in love. Love drives out fear completely.

If there is fear, there is not love.

Looking back to that moment in 2000, there was a lot of fear in my life. I'd survived, traversed, and denied eleven assaults and robberies perpetrated against me over the past twelve years. My DNA had become hardwired for self-defense, my danger-sensing radar always on high alert, but I was ferociously committed to not letting fear define my life. Even though living in Chicago scared me every day—walking to my car at night, looking over my shoulder while turning my key in the lock of my apartment door, listening for footsteps behind me—I still loved the energy and vibrancy of the city.

Passport packed and headed to LA to join a group of people I didn't know very well for two weeks in the poverty of Mexico was one more act of defiance against the fear. At LAX we rented two vans, piled in gear and people, then headed to a warehouse just this side of Tijuana, filled with supplies from churches and community groups intended for the orphanages over the border. As mission groups head south, they stop at the warehouse to pick up soap, shampoo, and other much-needed hygiene and living supplies. Somehow, we missed the memo to bring one critical item: lots of rope.

Both vans were equipped with steel racks plugged into the trailer hitch sockets and bar racks on the roofs, but we had nothing to tie the bags and boxes of supplies to the vans and we were filled to overflowing inside with our own gear. Rummaging through the warehouse, I found a large roll of industrial strength trash bags. At that time in my life, I was racing all over the world, and one thing I never left at home was my trusted Gerber multi-tool which holds a screwdriver, knife, file, and pliers. A girl needs her tool kit with her at all times. I've also carried one in my glove compartment for over thirty years, and I use it!

Armed with the Gerber, we could turn that roll of trash bags into rope! Soon, an assembly line was in place, and four people unfurled and held the corners of the trash bags while I slashed them into one-and-a-half inch strips. We must have dissected over fifty trash bags. Others enthusiastically braided the strips, making over 200 feet of rope in half an hour. This gave us enough to lash the boxes and bags onto the back and top of our vans.

We just had to get through border patrol, which at that time was not a foregone conclusion. We'd been told that border crossings were haphazard, depending on the whim of the overworked, under-compensated individual in the small booth. On good days you could be waved through without much of a look at your driver's ID. Other days, vehicles were pulled over and a thorough search delayed the journey. On really bad days, entry was denied for no cause.

With hope and trepidation, we produced our passports; the guards took a quick look around our vehicles, inside and out, and waved us through. Abby shouted, "Praise God," when we crossed into Mexico. I didn't see what the big deal was. Don't get me wrong, I have faith that God and love can heal what is broken, but praying for shampoo and conditioner to get across the border seemed contrived.

It was much later in the trip when I heard the story of the recent three failed attempts to take supplies through this same border crossing. That gave me a glimpse of the level of faith people relied on for the most basic things in life. The children and staff at the mission had been waiting and praying for a month for soap to get to them. One mission group canceled the week before their scheduled arrival, another had been turned away at the border and had to take everything back to the warehouse, and the third made it through, only to be accosted at a gas station in the Baja and have all the supplies stolen. So, a multipurpose tool, some innovative teamwork, and a relaxed border guard truly were an answer to prayer.

We drove through the gate. The mission was comprised of a compound of sand-colored buildings. Rolling to a stop in front of a playground with brightly painted equipment, gleeful children jumped off teeter-totters and swing sets and began to surround us. Staff welcomed us with open arms as we piled out of the vans into a sea of joy and laughter.

We had arrived at Foundations For His Ministry, and Abby Jill was the angel superhero bringing workers and supplies all the way from Chicago.

The staff quickly prepared a hot meal of tortillas and rice, which the older children served as we laughed. We joined in singing while holding gleeful, wriggling little girls and boys in our laps. My heart felt full. There was so much joy in the room. Work, bills, city chaos, and cold weather were far away. There we were, ready to serve, build friendships, and bring hope.

I was told at a young age that it is more blessed to give than to receive. But I have always found it to be that, when serving others, I get more than I give. It makes me wonder: does that really make it selfless, or a quid pro quo? Later in life, after showing up to help in places of great need, I've come to realize that giving isn't transactional; it's a win, win, win. Those we are serving benefit, we are more fulfilled, and something is made better in the world. But in that moment, as I sat there eating tortillas with the children, I felt I was receiving all the giving.

It was time to clear our plates and do the dishes. With soapy water up to my elbows, I looked up to read the large sign hanging over the sink. In twelve-inch red letters, "Your Life Will Never Be the Same."

Darcy and I were paired as roommates, and we couldn't have been more opposite. To say that Darcy, the high-powered LA talent agent, was out of her comfort zone would be an understatement. But the mission field is an equalizer. Ironically, much like sailing. It doesn't matter what your day job is, who your parents are, or how much money you make; when we are on the boat it's all about the job at hand. And the gnarlier the weather conditions get, the less anything on the outside of that boat and the racecourse matters.

Our rooms were clean but radically simple: two cots, each with a two-inch mattress, sheet, blanket, pillow, and a small dresser to share. A single window filtered the dusty afternoon sun. Bathrooms were in a different building, and I would soon become intimately acquainted with them.

After breakfast and singing that fueled my soul, our first day of serving began. Darcy and I were assigned to clean the bathrooms and we set off with a bucket of soapy water in one hand and a toilet brush in the other.

When faced with the prospect of cleaning a public toilet, I had to work through some "head trash" to get rid of thoughts like: *This is beneath me, gross. I can be put to better use.* That's the noise that screamed through my thoughts as I struggled to be fully present in the moment of serving. Then it hit me hard, that I had a choice to be there scrubbing a toilet. Unlike the single mother holding down three jobs, who has to do this every day to feed her family, I would go back to my upwardly mobile life at the end of the trip. Head trash gone. Kneeling on a bathroom floor with someone is a great way to get to know them. Darcy shared a bit about her life, which gave us a base for much more storytelling throughout the week.

Later in the afternoon, with many chores behind us, we walked down to the ocean. In the Baja it is possible to walk along the beach for miles without seeing another soul. I felt enveloped in the safe, beautiful arms of the sand, warm breeze, and waves. We sang, shared moments from the day, and were grateful for our joy and for one another.

The next morning, we divided up into new teams and ventured outside the compound. With Ken behind the wheel, Lisa riding shotgun, and me bouncing around in the back, we headed down a dirt road to a small village, an enclave of shacks made from corrugated sheet metal, covered in plywood. Our task was to drive our van into the village and invite the children to come see us—like an ice cream truck without the music. They knew who we were and what we were bringing, and they immediately poured out of their yards and lean-tos and ran to see us. They smelled—a sharp, raw, acrid stench, strong enough to make my eyes water. But that didn't stop the hugs. We picked the children up and some wrapped their arms around our necks as we trotted around the van.

We handed each smiling, grimy child a plastic cup filled with milk, which they held in both hands. Lisa dipped a spoon in a vat of peanut butter and placed gooey dollops in the cups. Big smiles shone on grimy faces as they each grabbed their spoon and rushed the peanut butter into their happy mouths.

Then we pulled out something they hadn't seen before—small yellow boxes that we pointed in their direction. It took a bit of broken Spanish and sign language to get them to understand that we wanted them to be still and smile. After a click sound, a piece of paper slid out of the box. Impatiently, they gathered around us to see what would happen and squealed as they saw themselves, some for the first time, in the photographs.

It was a little hard to comprehend as we weren't deep in the wilds of the Amazon or Saharan Africa, but only three hours from the US border; neither Polaroid cameras nor film had reached the village. Few had ever seen their own likeness.

Ken motioned for Lisa and me to stand with one of the small boys. Filthy blue shirt, baggy, faded shorts, and barefooted, he beamed toward the yellow box and waited for the click. Once the picture was taken, our little friend immediately ran to Ken, where he stood patiently in front of him and waited for the magic picture to appear on the paper. But as the print developed, I saw Ken's eyebrow raise with a look of concern. He said to me, "The picture didn't work. We need to take it again."

Lisa put her arms around our blue-shirted friend and pulled him back into our embrace for another click. This time Ken placed the picture into the boy's outstretched hands and gave him a high five. As the boy walked away, I asked Ken what had happened to the first photo. Shaking, he pulled the photo from his back pocket. As the three of us looked at the picture, my heart stopped. I felt a cold fear. There, above the little boy, between Lisa and me was a dark, hazy, ominous, tall shape. It was too distinct to be a Polaroid film error, human but not human. It just stood there between us, looming over our little friend. The image felt evil.

Speechless, we held each other and started praying for protection, for the little boy, his friends, and for ourselves. As I stood on unsteady legs, I finally remembered my verse, "There is no fear in Love. Love drives out fear completely."

At home in all the modern comforts, feeling safe with our locked doors and patrol cars on the street, with good work and convenience a priority for much of the day, we do not often experience overwhelming joy and peace. And while there is the potential for violence around the corner, we rarely feel and see evil—raw evil. There is almost always something to buffer the joy and protect us from the terror.

In much of the Baja, amidst widespread poverty, alcohol-fueled domestic abuse, drugs, and abandonment, the comforts of life are few. Survival and safety are the focus. Fear is high and hope is low. In this stark environment the sun shines more brightly, the waves are bluer, and the atrocities feel more heinous.

Prayer at home is a personal thing, and something we do together before meals and in church on Sunday. On the front lines of good and evil, in that place of little safety, prayer was a real protector. It calmed our fear, kept us focused on hope, and called on the good to battle the darkness. Do I know what that dread-producing image was in the photo? No. I do know that it invoked an instant feeling of danger and the motivation to protect the children and ourselves. Without guns, police, or even doors we could run behind and lock, we prayed.

Four days later, as I stood at the top of the escalator in LAX, I was overwhelmed by this thought: *I had a choice.* I had the power to choose what this trip meant to me. It could be a learning experience that gave me a huge feeling of love and joy from serving, together with memories supported by a few photos of our meaningful moments. I could go back to work on Monday morning feeling good about what I had done. And as the sign above the sink in the kitchen challenged, "My Life Will Never Be the Same."

During the weeks and months that followed, there were days that I felt grateful for the heart-stretching memories and the new friendships forged in our travel and serving together. It was indeed a vacation with purpose. But then something would trigger me: a late-night walk to my car, finding myself alone late in my office, encountering a stranger who didn't make me feel safe; the fear would return, raw and cold. In Mexico I had experienced another level of darkness in the world. One without a face. What was I going to do about it? How was I going to protect the children? How could I fight the darkness? What light did I possess that would turn back the presence of evil?

These questions have haunted me for decades. I am forced to wrestle with them every time I step into the unknown, read a story of some atrocity committed against the vulnerable or find myself out-side of my comfort zone. Rather than being a burden, these questions are a call to action and encourage me to "do something." Because in that little enclave, holding a small boy, jubilant over a spoonful of peanut butter, I experienced first-hand that showing up in love is enough and prayer works.

Prayer works when miles separate us. Prayer works when we don't know how to help.

Prayer works even when we don't know how to pray.

16

WHY CAN'T YOU BE BAD AT THIS?

KELLY WEST

"WHY CAN'T YOU BE bad at this?"

Those were my words immediately following my first kiss with Mike. It wasn't that I didn't want to be in a relationship; it was just that I had reservations about being in a relationship with someone eight years younger than me. I was already wondering how I would explain our age difference.

That first kiss melted those worries—and a lot of other worries—away. Everything just clicked. I'd manifested him. I didn't realize it until later in our relationship, but when you know, you know. He was everything on my list and more.

My list was more cut-to-the-chase than physical attributes like ideal height and hair color. He needed a deep sense of humor and to love me for me—whether I was dressed for a night out or in my workout gear.

I was blissful. Even better, so was he. Everyone we met could see our strong connection. And I realized how much of a train wreck all my other relationships had been—which is why I was (and still am) unbelievably grateful that our paths crossed, even for such a brief time.

You see, Mike was my husband for only one week.

Mike and I loved spending time together, doing everything and anything, and we quickly decided to travel. Mike was an amateur filmmaker and wanted to make a documentary about his family. Because of Mike's roots in Italy (and a connection to the family that created the zeppole pastry), we booked a cruise to Italy and Greece, with plans to stop at a bakery still bearing the family name, hoping to get footage for his film. Our bags were packed, and we were extremely excited about our first major trip.

I want to tell you our trip was amazing—but the trip never happened. Instead, we spent the weekend in the hospital trying to determine why Mike's balance was off.

We'd soon learn that brain cancer was the reason.

In one weekend, our lives changed drastically. Instead of exploring Italy and Greece, we were figuring out just what this diagnosis meant. Well, not only that weekend, but starting that weekend ... and running through the remainder of Mike's life—which was about eighteen months.

Mike and I remained inseparable through doctor's appointments and regular MRI scans and all the mundane activities of daily life. Although this diagnosis was the worst news that a happy couple could get, we remained positive that Mike's case would be different—even if we both knew there was little chance.

It was a year of extreme highs and extreme lows. We even bought a house in the middle of the chaos! Little did we know the memories we'd make over the next eleven months in that house.

We moved into our home in January of 2015. In August, Mike was diagnosed with another brain tumor on the other side of his brain. This new tumor was much more aggressive than the first, and affected him neurologically. Mike's health declined rapidly; this was devastating to us both, and to those who loved us.

Mike's parents came to visit from Florida to help me care for him. To make the situation even more devastating, my mother passed away unexpectedly in October. After my mother passed, my father came over daily to help as well. Care for Mike was becoming more challenging, as he could no longer walk and had begun to lose his ability to speak.

It's said that "God doesn't give you any more than you can handle." Well, He must have been testing my limits.

About a week after my mother passed, I had a very frank conversation with Mike's neurologist, since Mike's tumor wasn't responding to treatment. I asked, "Should we consider halting treatment and looking into hospice care?"

After a long pause, the neurologist quietly said, "If Mike were my loved one, I would."

I talked to Mike about that conversation, and he agreed. I'd already decided on in-home hospice care since I knew Mike hated hospitals and I refused to allow his last days to be in a place he hated. A friend's wife works at a local hospice, and so I called her. She immediately got the ball rolling and within a day, we had a caseworker and hospice nurse in our home explaining the process.

The caseworker and hospice nurse met first with me and Mike's mom to review what to expect and how to keep Mike comfortable as the cancer progressed. After, she spoke with Mike and me to explain the process to him. Although Mike had lost the ability to speak, he hadn't lost his ability to comprehend. At this point, he communicated with one hand, pointing to a giant keyboard that we'd made from poster board. He conveyed he understood what was happening and what to expect. When the caseworker and nurse left, we just held each other and cried.

The next morning, I woke up and started doing what had been our routine for the past few weeks—get up, get myself showered, and then get Mike washed and dressed for the day. This day, Mike was pointing toward the keyboard, obviously needing to deliver a message. As he started pointing to each letter, it was clear he was spelling out "iPad."

Mike's vision was also starting to fail, so I asked him what he needed his iPad for, since it had been a source of frustration the last time he attempted to use something with such small print. He then started pointing out the letters for "credit card." That he was even contemplating some sort of purchase was strange to me. Perplexed, I asked him what he was looking to buy. After what seemed like a game of charades, he finally communicated that he wanted to marry me and wanted to buy me a ring!

Overwhelmed with emotion, I asked him if I had understood correctly what he had communicated. He confirmed.

I could not have loved him more at that moment. This was the last thing he wanted to do—make our union official.

I called the caseworker and asked if there was an officiant available to marry us. Within a few days, we arranged for our wedding to take place in our living room, surrounded by only our immediate family and friends that are like family. For the ring, my father suggested my mother's wedding band and engagement ring. Mike and I loved the idea and by using her ring, it felt like my mother was with us that day.

Our house absorbed all the love of two soulmates from our beautiful wedding in our living room in mid-November. One week later, the love in those walls supported me through the loss of Mike in the exact place we were married. Strangely enough, our cat Sylvester sometimes lies in that exact spot. I wonder if he still feels Mike's energy—I know I do.

I never, ever thought that I would become a widow at forty-four years old. As I navigated to figure out how to deal with my grief and heal, my path crossed with a woman who'd formed a foundation to raise funds for brain cancer research, the Amy Gallagher Foundation. Armed with all the momentum to make a difference, and craving a purpose, I donated my time to this foundation to help plan her annual gala. I did not foresee my front-row seat to my newfound friend Amy experiencing the same decline that Mike went through just over a year earlier.

Heartbreak, chapter two.

As I planned the annual gala with a small committee of Amy's friends, the reality of her grim situation continued to set in. All the physical and emotional changes that one experiences when diagnosed with a life-ending disease like brain cancer were evident during my weekly interactions with Amy. It became harder and harder to keep a smile on my face when I could see the consistent decline in Amy's health.

The echo of Mike's life got louder and louder every time an additional symptom of cancer took another one of Amy's abilities away. I refused to walk away, but how could I deal with the stress of planning a gala that I knew would be her last, while coping with the decline of a dear friend?

The answer? Sunday morning yoga with Grace.

It was through my yoga practice that I learned how to turn my awareness inward and give myself the self-care time I needed with some help from Grace. The funny thing is, she has no idea the impact her yoga class had on me. I had done yoga throughout the years, but had always been more of a gym girl who preferred indoor cycling classes and weight training to the slow flow of a yoga class. During this time though, something in me just craved the therapy of a well-led yoga class, not to work the body but to calm the mind. As I continued to benefit from Grace's wisdom through her yoga instruction, my mind wanted to learn more about yoga philosophy and the effect the practice can have on mental and emotional health. It also occurred to me I still had plenty of grieving to do.

Yoga Teacher Training was a rigorous six months of training. Once my training was complete, I began teaching yoga at the same gym where I taught indoor cycling classes. The challenge was to offer the type of yoga that benefits the mind before benefiting the body. It was a tough concept to introduce to those looking only to work out their body in a gym setting.

After some time, I convinced some brave souls to trust me with this yoga that heals the mind and then the body. When you synchronize your movement to your breath and allow your body to slow down and feel the movement and breath, an interesting thing happens. Your nervous system responds. It settles down. It allows your mind to catch up and—if you are lucky—release its thoughts.

People in my classes were feeling the difference between how they felt when they walked into class—hyped up from their day—and how they felt after an hour of mindfully moving their bodies and slowing their breathing. The difference was visible, whether they'd floated off their mat or the stress lines disappeared from their face.

Why yoga? How could I have found something as basic, yet complex, as yoga practice to help me heal and deal with life's twists and turns? I choose to share this ancient practice with other people because of my discovery. It's saved me and I've seen it save others as well. Every time I teach a class, it heals me just a little bit more. Yoga is just too powerful to keep to myself. That is my "why."

Nowadays, I teach at a fitness studio that allows and encourages the mind and body connection experience, understanding that it isn't only beneficial to provide training for maintaining the body, but also necessary to provide training for managing the mind as well. Through these weekly classes, I can not only provide this important practice for others but also continue to fill my cup by doing the work that I love so much. In my corporate career, when I am not working as a senior systems analyst, I serve as the Wellness Committee chairperson where I offer the occasional meditation session, cycling, or yoga class at every opportunity . Every bit counts.

There is a famous quote from Mahatma Gandhi: "Be the change you wish to see in the world." I have always resonated with this quote, but never really knew why. I now know: I was meant to share the value and benefits of this ancient practice with others so they may also use it as a tool to help heal the wounds of life's journey.

This year marks seven years that Mike has been gone. His passing has helped me to find purpose and gratitude where there once loomed hopelessness and bitterness. I am forever grateful to him for touching my life.

Rise into

GRACE

17

SURRENDER, TRUST, BELIEVE

CHRISTINE GALLO

MY BOYS HAVE A MOM, my husband has a wife, my parents have a daughter, my siblings have a sister, and my family and friends have Christine. With certainty, I can say none of them realized just how close they came to losing her—how she felt she had run out of options. In fact, she would not be here today if I hadn't made the decision that saved her life on that Monday morning in May 2017.

***

As I drove to the elementary school where I'd taught for the past seventeen years, I felt stronger than I had in months. I'd returned from a weekend away, spending time in self-reflection, reading, and resetting my state of mind. Once again, I had convinced myself that I was in control of my thoughts and feelings, and that I had all the tools I needed to keep myself from slipping again. No longer would I spend emotional and mental energy on situations that ultimately were beyond my influence. I wouldn't allow them to consume me anymore.

I turned off my radio and started speaking my mantras and affirmations out loud, the first steps of a drive-into-work ritual that I'd begun months prior.

Arriving at school, I parked in my regular spot, as far from the building as I could, put on the Mrs. Gallo mask I'd perfected, shut my car off, and centered my breath. I purposefully and mindfully walked toward the building, grounding myself with each step. My heart was open, my mind was clear, and I was ready.

After I greeted the first person in the parking lot, before I even entered the building, the strength I'd felt minutes earlier was gone, and I was empty. Physically. Emotionally. Mentally. Completely depleted. The thought that I'd never be better returned. No matter what I did, I knew I would feel like this forever. I had nothing left.

I finally made it to the safety of my classroom and shut the door behind me. I just needed to make it to 9:15 a.m. to take the kids to their special. Then, I could hide in the bathroom and cry. If I could get through the next forty-five minutes, I'd have a moment to break down and then enough time to put my Mrs. Gallo mask back on. It was the only way to survive the rest of the day.

I have no idea what I said or how I managed, but I called on all the strength I had.

When the moment I'd been holding out for finally arrived, I felt so relieved. However, when I opened my door to walk my kids to their class, I was shocked to find my husband waiting outside my classroom. Apparently, he had something to drop off and was coming to my room to visit. My husband was one of a few people who could see through my Mrs. Gallo mask, and he waited in my classroom for my return.

At that moment, I knew I was done. I needed to walk away.

To see him there at my door after holding on for that moment, I knew I was being shown what I must live for. My career was killing me, and my love for my family would save me. I couldn't ignore any longer the realization that I had no choice but to leave.

If I stayed, I would die.

My entire life, I've lived with suicidal ideations and thoughts of self-harm. I remember becoming aware that other people didn't have intrusive thoughts like mine when I would share what was an everyday thought to me and see the shocked looks on their faces. After that, I learned to keep my daily thoughts to myself.

These thoughts came out of nowhere. They were vivid and detailed, but rational to me. Whenever I would get to really dark places—which was often—the thought of suicide wasn't frightening. Instead, it was almost comforting. I had plans, and knew exactly what I would do.

However, specific thoughts prevented me from acting on my impulses. The thought of someone living with the guilt that they missed a sign and could've helped me. Realizing someone would find me, and how hard the first responders would work to save my life, and what they would go through if I didn't make it. If I went elsewhere to do the deed, my family would be forced to endure the journey to bring me home. As my kids grew, I could see how happy, smart, and well-adjusted they were; with my death, their joy would die, changing the course of their lives. That final reason is the one that I kept returning to. I couldn't do that to my kids, and I couldn't do that to my husband.

Throughout the years, I tried many things to help with my depression, although the tremendous guilt and shame I felt only exacerbated it. In my head, I had no reason to feel such heaviness, and I was embarrassed that I couldn't will myself out of it. My friends and family were supportive and loving. I was well-educated, healthy, and financially stable. I was physically active, regularly practiced yoga and meditation, went to therapy, and took daily medication.

I did *all the right things.*

After both of my boys were born, I had severe postpartum depression, which elevated the depressive thoughts I'd lived with for years to a level that I didn't know was possible. All my previous tools for regulating my depression needed adjustment because they stopped working.

When my second son was around two years old, I signed up for my first "Out of the Darkness Overnight Walk" with the American Foundation for Suicide Prevention. Everyone thought this walk was in memory of a college friend of mine who died by suicide when I was serving in the Peace Corps. She was a happy, laughing, sweet girl who always had a smile and a kind word for everyone. She radiated light and warmth, which she readily gave away, but couldn't keep for herself; I walked in her name, but it was really for me. If I died by suicide, I knew I would leave people with those same thoughts of me, unable to reconcile their memories of me with the way I left the world. I needed to see people and to hear stories from those who loved someone they lost—those left behind—to make me want to stay. I needed to remind myself what leaving would do to the people I loved.

For many years, I did this walk as a yearly reset, and loved it every time.

During the last few years of my career, I could feel my mental health rapidly deteriorating. Since I was in second grade, I'd known that I'd be a teacher, and I loved teaching, children, and learning. Staff and parents respected me and sought me out, and people knew how much I loved my job. My smile and my love made my students' days better, and I knew I was making a difference. I poured all of myself into my job and was emotionally invested in the lives of my students. I put the same amount of effort into making my school a better place. Also, I helped with leadership: I was team leader, led many committees that I thought would help people, and volunteered time to help staff and the kids. I felt good about my contribution, and I loved knowing that my smile was making other people's days better.

The thing was, my smile, although genuine, was becoming harder to find every day. In the morning, I didn't wake up with that smile, and I didn't go to sleep at night with it. Every day, I gave everything away to those around me. I wasn't saving enough for myself or my family.

After a sleepless night filled with panic attacks thinking about other people's children and the infuriating situations in my school, I fought to get out of bed each morning, sick to my stomach, and in tears. Most days, I cried nearly the whole ride to school. I loved teaching, but the stress of the negative work environment, the politics, the constant fighting for what I knew was right for my students, the knowledge that I had a limited amount of time with them, and

that there were so many factors in their lives causing so much sadness ... all these factors were stealing my love of teaching away from
me. I was burned out, and all the boundaries I'd created to protect
me and my family were no longer working.

The stress, which for years had only affected me mentally and
emotionally, was now showing physically. My hair fell out, I developed rashes and allergies, and my menstrual cycle became very
heavy. I lost weight rapidly and underwent multiple tests for various
diseases, which all came back negative. What was affecting my body
was my mental health.

By the time I knew I had to leave teaching, all my resources
were depleted. I was doing everything I could to make changes, but
nothing had a lasting effect. The moments where I truly felt happy
or joyful without a hint of anxiety and sadness were fleeting. When
I recognized I was feeling happy, I would immediately feel sad I
couldn't be that way more often. I wanted the weeks and the school
year to pass as fast as possible and was wishing time away. I lived for
Saturdays, Sunday mornings, and July, when I could be in my home
with my husband and my boys, the only time I felt at all alive.

I woke up in tears on Mondays, did my best to get through the
days, left everything I had in my classroom, and couldn't wait to get
back in bed. I hung on by a thread to make it to Friday when I could
come home and not have to be on stage for a few days.

Saturdays were good, but as soon as we finished lunch on Sunday,
I was back in my depressive state. I never wanted to do anything on
Sunday and tried to nap as much as possible. That way, I was still
home with my family, but they didn't have to see what a mess I was
and my mood wouldn't affect them. It was much easier to have them

think I was exhausted rather than show my emptiness. I was wasting time away, watching my boys get older and missing out on being present in their lives.

That Monday morning was the ultimate test. My angels, my ancestors, and my spirit guides—those who were always looking out for me—gave me a clear message. It was time to go. It was time to surrender, and trust the decision I was making was the right one. What I had to live for was waiting for me at my classroom door and represented everything waiting for me at home. Everything would work out if I trusted I was being divinely guided.

So, I left my career and my identity as Mrs. Gallo, and began the process of finding Christine.

***

In the fall of 2022, my sister and I led a yoga and mindfulness retreat in Iceland. Sitting on the cliffs of Hrisey Island, overlooking the mountains and the Arctic Circle, feeling grounded to the earth, centered in my body, and connected to my higher power, I cried. The release was overwhelming. I became lost in feelings of immense gratitude and recognition of how my life has been transformed—how I am fully living my truth and trusting my intuition to guide me. I know that I am always being led to choices that allow me to be the best version of myself for those around me. There is an awareness of feeling whole and complete, knowing I can serve others without losing myself.

And it has all happened because, on a Monday in May of 2017, I chose to *live*.

The Icelanders have a phrase: *petta reddast.* Loosely translated, it means, "Trust that it will all work out in the end." I do.

18

SPIRITUAL SURGERY

FELICIA MESSINA D'HAITI

"OH, MY GOD! You're going to let them take your *womb*?"

Before she even finished her exclamation, my friend's words shocked me.

I thought I stood firm in my official decision; however, those words ignited a tiny spark of lingering doubt. Was I making the right decision? Was this surgery really necessary, or was I taking too drastic of a step? Maybe I was taking the fast road by not pursuing other, more subtle options. I wasn't sure. Yet, my treatment options were dwindling quickly. For years I might as well have lived in the doctor's office with all my visits for scans and other smaller, less invasive surgeries and procedures. I knew I had to do *something*.

The previous two years, especially, were filled with pain and discomfort. I'd already been through two different cancer diagnoses along with their accompanying treatments of multiple surgeries, chemotherapy to treat colon cancer, and radiation to treat breast cancer. Yet, the daily pain and discomfort I felt from my lower abdomen and back was overwhelming compared to those earlier journeys. It crept up on me, enveloped me, and trapped me into a daily experience of uneasiness. I could no longer count on experiencing a pain-free day, and I no longer expected one either. My lower back and uterus took turns feeling constricted, compressed, and twisted. Sometimes it felt as if my entire lower torso were being crushed in a weird, medieval torture device. My physical body felt sore and worn out.

What I didn't understand at the time was that the energetic weight from the pain, discomfort, and unpredictable bleeding was suppressing my spirit.

My numerous visits to the doctor's office provided little relief. Scan after scan, they couldn't find a definitive cause for the pain other than a few small fibroids—and some doctors didn't believe the fibroids could cause the pain I described. During those two years, I underwent a few minor medical procedures that I and my doctors hoped would alleviate the pain and heavy bleeding. The results, though, were extremely disappointing. After the last procedure, the pain even got worse. The severity of the pain continued to increase each month, and I experienced longer and more intense menstrual cycles—often multiple times in a month and so lasting for most of it.

I felt weighed down by the pain, and yet, with its constant presence every day, it became part of who I was. Daily, I was exhausted, nervous that I might start bleeding unexpectedly, tired of taking medicine all the time, and just simply uncomfortable in and with my body. My body's discomfort, especially after my two experiences with cancer, reinforced the idea that I could no longer rely on my physical body to operate without some level of pain. And this belief weighed heavily on my spirit. I hesitated to make plans, never knowing how I was going to feel, not knowing if I would need to pack an extra pair of clothes in case of "accidents," and always thinking of contingency and emergency plans to make sure I had all the feminine supplies I could possibly need at any given moment. With the uncertainty of it all, I felt somehow separate from my body, as if we were no longer working as one. This experience became another part of my journey during which I felt like my body was failing me.

On one of my phone consultations with the doctor, she reiterated they didn't find a definitive cause for my pain, nor did they find any sign of cancer, which was a concern. She offered that since the other minor procedures hadn't worked, I could choose to have a hysterectomy. Her suggestion was an interesting one for me. While listening to her talk, I realized nobody had given me that option before. I found myself in a place where the surgery wasn't an emergency, there was no clear diagnosis, and I was given an option to decide if I wanted to have major surgery.

Six years earlier, when doctors discovered advanced stage colon cancer, I barely had time to think about anything. It was a two-week whirlwind of events, from the discovery of the cancer to the surgery, where they removed the cancer along with my ascending colon. I found that I was following instructions in a haze more than making major decisions. This was an entirely new experience.

In this case, the doctor put the entire decision in my lap.

She simply said, "If you want the pain to be gone, have the surgery. But it's not an emergency nor a mandate, so you can take your time to choose what you're most comfortable with." There was no definitive diagnosis other than some small fibroids. So, what was the choice I was most comfortable with?

Knowing that my body had been through a great deal in the previous six years, when the most serious operation I had before that was the removal of my wisdom teeth, I resisted volunteering for major surgery with its myriad potential complications. But I still felt called to say yes despite being terrified.

A million questions popped into my mind. What if I made the wrong decision? It's not as if they could put my uterus back in my body. What if the back pain persisted? Or if I developed other pains or issues as a result of the surgery? During my decision-making process, I realized I could no longer remember what it was like to live without pain, nor was I confident that I could ever be pain free again.

I was also piecing together the parts of myself that I'd ignored in order to deal with the never-ending pain. It wasn't simply my physical state of being that was suffering. The mental, emotional and spiritual aspects of my being also suffered. While focused on bringing myself to a place where I was no longer in pain, I put many things on the back burner. There were events I did not attend, projects that I did not finish as I moved through and with the pain. As a result of being so focused on pain mitigation, I let other activities and practices wither. Not much else, not even some of my favorite things like writing, teaching, and traveling, seemed fun anymore.

Deep inside, I felt I was making the best choice despite all my questions. When additional doubts arose, I countered them by acknowledging that my uterus had done its job. I'd given birth to four beautiful children, including a set of twins. It had never failed me and certainly worked seamlessly earlier in my life. Now, at just over fifty years old, I was definitely not planning to have any more children. Accepting that the decision was in my hands, I could more deeply process that I was releasing a part of my body for the overall wellness of my whole being.

Using some ideas from friends and the internet, I created a gratitude and releasing ceremony for my uterus. I thanked my uterus for holding and nurturing life and for being an integral part of my body and my being. I also acknowledged the sadness and grief I was experiencing for releasing another part of my body. I was stepping into the unknown, trusting that this was the best choice for me.

As I sat with my decision and approached the surgery, I still had no idea how this "Yes!" would reverberate through everything and shift my life.

On the Friday of Easter weekend, the day of my surgery arrived, and I was full of positive expectations. My hysterectomy went smoothly and the surgeon was pleased. Although it seemed like a long time before I could sit up straight in a chair again, I healed well and in good time. Six weeks after surgery, when I visited my doctor for a follow-up, I was feeling surprisingly well. I was actually feeling beyond wonderful!

While I had not noticed it during the first six weeks, as I transitioned back to work and family events, I realized my body moved more easily and freely. I didn't have to constantly adjust myself when sitting or driving. I wasn't moving as if I needed to protect my back or front. Then, gradually, I became aware that I was no longer experiencing discomfort in my body. Nor was I in constant pain. I felt like a miracle had occurred. I experienced a new lightness and a new sense of physical freedom.

Once I began enjoying my new physical state of being, I also saw how deeply entrenched my physical pain had been prior to surgery. The pain and discomfort had blended into the background of my daily experiences, and to live my life, I'd needed massive amounts of energy to physically function. I understood how deeply exhausting it had been. My new reality was foreign to me. What was this new grace and ease with which I moved? It was a wonderful yet unfamiliar feeling to wake up in the morning, get out of bed, and not immediately grab to brace my back or comfort my abdomen.

And yet, much more than the physical transformation, I experienced a new lightness of being. It felt like the surgery had released my mind and spirit from a prison, and they could now wander freely with a sense of joy and peace. It was as if I had a ball of creativity that had been imprisoned within a cage—and then, unexpectedly, the cage had been shattered. Having the hysterectomy in the spring was an incredible synchronicity. By the time I was back out in the world, it was nearly summer. A new me had been birthed during this springtime, and I was ready to play in a way that I had not done in quite some time.

Some of the changes are still difficult to capture in words. For example, there were indescribable energetic shifts noticeable in my approach to life. The relief had reignited my attitude of positive expectancy. I returned to things I loved but hadn't been up to for the past few years because I didn't feel well. I felt a lightness in my spirit and was more joyful. I also embraced a new freedom, releasing my supplies of tampons and pads, special "leak proof" underwear, and more. I was moving and operating in ways I hadn't in several years. Friends even noticed a change in me.

This surgery experience has taught me the power of standing in my "Yes!" despite my fears and doubts. Despite other people's reactions and opinions, I chose what was best for me. And when I deeply listen to what my body is telling me, I will always make the right choice. When it comes from a place of love and honoring of self, any choice I make is the best next step for me. The most loving choice I could've made for myself was one that supported my well-being. Even now, several months after surgery, I have no regrets; I know I didn't let anyone take anything from me!

Through my hysterectomy experience, I learned to love all parts of myself, especially the ones that need healing. Here, I was able to bless and express gratitude for all the physical parts of myself that I had to release over the last six years. I honored my transformation and my body's remarkable ability to heal.

Sometimes in the past, I felt my body had betrayed me, and I didn't feel love and gratitude for my body or myself. But here, in this time and space, I was inspired to love my body and myself and to be grateful for all of me. In doing so, I could reclaim and rejoice in the energetic parts of myself that hadn't flourished while I was focused on the tasks of functioning while in such pain and discomfort.

This experience reignited my self-confidence and unbottled my creativity. It's as if my physical uterus had been clogging up the energetic flow in my body and spirit. Now I am free to express my creativity. I am empowered to stand in my choices while knowing that I can make a new choice at any time. I am more "me" than I have ever been before.

19

ASK ME TOMORROW

MARY JANE MILICI

I WAS GOING ON THIRTEEN when I got my first pair of pointe shoes. These beautiful, light pink, silk shoes are a ballerina's rite of passage, and though they look like pure elegance, they also symbolize hours upon hours of torturous, painstaking work. I coveted those shoes from a young age and, holding them in my hands at thirteen, I felt as though a brand-new journey lay ahead.

At that point, dancing had consumed a large part of my life. I have memories and home videos of myself skipping across the dance studio floor in a tutu and tiny ballet slippers, barely able to reach the barre. As I grew older, dancing became addicting, taking over my life but also giving me life. The director of my dance company pulled me aside at one point to tell me I had potential, and it filled me with thrill and determination.

There can be no denying that ballet is a rigorous form of exercise, but it was around the age of thirteen that, discouragingly, I started to feel winded or even lightheaded after a jump sequence. I would need to excuse myself to the bathroom and press a cold paper towel to the back of my neck and forehead. Perhaps this was the first sign that something was wrong, but I kept remembering what the director said, and it pushed me to continue. I was aware I could not lift my leg the highest, but I made sure to perform every combination with elegance despite any frustration.

I wanted to do good. I yearned for it.

My favorite season was Nutcracker Season—a tradition kept between me and my mother. The season starts in September and goes through early December. It includes long hours of practice, fun, and a little magic. Since the age of eight, I auditioned each year for the Island Moving Company's production of *The Nutcracker*, which is an immersive performance where the audience follows the dancers from room to room in the historic Rosecliff Mansion. To be eight years old and performing in this space was captivating. I was ecstatic to be backstage among the older dancers who seemed far more advanced, though they were really just teenagers.

Then, suddenly, I became an older dancer, finding myself running back and forth for costume changes. Up and down stairs, adrenaline pumping and out of breath. I absolutely loved to perform the story of *The Nutcracker* and had dreams of one day achieving the lead role of Clara, but little did I know that 2013 would be my last year of ballet. My body simply could not keep up anymore. Not in class or any future rehearsals.

To this day, nearly ten years later, I still get a little nostalgic when I hear Tchaikovsky's music around Christmastime. As for my pointe shoes—newly achieved right around the end of 2013—they still sit pristinely in my closet.

Parallel to my world of dance was life at middle school. It was during seventh-grade English class that a boy randomly blurted, "MJ, your wrists are *disgusting*." There was no response, even from the teacher. I still remember his name and face—it seems most people do with their first bully. That was the same year I was asked if I was anorexic for the first time. People tend to describe me using three adjectives: tall, blonde, and skinny. I don't like the word "skinny," because it is always accompanied by the word "too." It is irritating that "skinny" always seems to be used in a derogatory way. I never really felt ashamed about my body until that year. I wanted to gain weight so people would stop calling me "too skinny," but by 2013, it became necessary.

Between often feeling lightheaded, easily getting tired, and my inability to gain weight, it seemed that something was wrong in my body. It was mutually agreed between doctors, my parents, and even—hesitantly—me, to go to a treatment facility at Hasbro Children's Hospital. Things remained vague at this point. I did not have an eating disorder, but doctor-logic thought otherwise, and the "treatment plan" was the same for all patients. Mealtime was quite absurd because every ounce on your plate had to be consumed. You were not allowed to use a napkin for fear that a smudge of peanut butter would stick to it. Not even a squirt of salad dressing could be left behind. If you left a butter packet untouched on your plate, they would make you unwrap it and swallow it while they watched. Any morsel left unconsumed meant that the equivalent of a supplement drink took its place. If that came back up, well, you had to try again. To this day, the smell of Ensure or Boost makes me queasy.

While this protocol did help me gain weight, I am not sure how forcing kids to shoot down ranch dressing will help them overcome an adverse relationship with eating.

High school was high school: a combination of good days and bad days, and any Mondays spent wishing it was Friday. Throughout these four years, I must say, I was quite fashionable with my cute all-gray outfits or white overalls. Yet, whether it was thirty or eighty degrees outside, I always wore a sweater. I would choose from my plethora of sweaters to derail any focus from my arms and wrists, always thinking of that comment from my middle school bully. I also despised gym class, an exhausting and humiliating endeavor that was required all four years. Basketball did not mesh well with my ballet training, and as you might have guessed, jumping is not my thing. I preferred the academic part of school. I was head of the Community Service Club and made it into the National Honors Society, Art Honors Society, and Language Honors Society (even though Spanish was my hardest class).

After high school I always intended to go to college, and eventually decided to attend Salve Regina University, which is about twenty-five minutes away from my home. So, when things eventually began to go awry, I was fortunate to be close by.

It first happened at an eighteen-plus club in Providence. I sat down to take a break from the loud music and fist-pumping, and I began to have psychedelic spots in my eyes. Then I went blind.

I mean *psychedelic*, as in the aesthetic of the transitions of *That '70s Show,* or when you blink after looking at the sun too long; *blind* as in wearing two eye patches—total darkness.

I was beyond fortunate that my friend came to sit with me through the first minutes of panic and confusion. Two more friends joined us, and we all climbed into the back of an Uber and asked to be taken to the Newport Hospital. The driver likely thought I was some high, drunk girl about to throw up a red Gatorade chaser. The receiving nurse certainly thought the same, until my blood came back clean. Call me paranoid, but I have never had the urge to drink or smoke. Nonetheless, by nineteen I would be taking so many medications and supplements that I would become a small celebrity at my local CVS.

In the hospital that first night, I regained my sight about five hours later. The first things I saw were my parents' concerned faces and my tired friends, still in their skimpy outfits and wrapped in those measly hospital blankets. The discharge papers stated it was a "complex acute ocular migraine"; in other words, no one knew what had really happened to me, and they were guessing.

When similar things began to occur a year later, I tried to sleep it off. Still, the migraines progressed until I found myself hanging over the toilet in the small bathroom of my triple dorm room. Then, I blacked out. I do not recall seizing on the bathroom floor, the two ambulance rides from one hospital to the other, or waking up. I use the term "waking up" loosely, as it was hazy and a little painful most of the time. I was in and out of consciousness. I have a memory of eating butterflies that tasted like salmon. After fifteen days at Brigham and Women's Hospital and a load of poking, prodding, and tests, doctors finally revealed the true culprit.

I have MELAS disease—Mitochondrial Encephalopathy, Lactic Acidosis, and Stroke-like symptoms. It is a specific type of genetic disease that prevents cells from absorbing or delivering enough energy to process properly. Depending on the number of cells affected in a specific area of the body, each individual person is affected differently with common symptoms of reduced energy, muscle weakness, difficulty walking, difficulty swallowing, and neurological symptoms. Mitochondrial diseases often manifest as neurological and/or metabolic conditions. (Um, bingo!)

While the stroke-like symptoms came on strong at nineteen, the signs of MELAS had been there all along, such as when I had to quit dance because I felt too weak, or when I'd had issues with gaining weight. It took years of telling doctors a repetitive story that things didn't feel right to get my diagnosis. I told them over and over that I was eating plenty and I was tired. Really, really tired. My story is not unique: mitochondrial diseases are complex and only discussed briefly in medical textbooks, so many people are misdiagnosed, sometimes for years.

My loss of vision is caused by little lesions that form after a seizure in the back of my brain, the cerebellum, which administers the function of the optic nerves. Otherwise, as confirmed by my ophthalmologist, I have 20/20 vision. Unlike that first grand mal seizure, I have been awake and aware through all the seizures since. The psychedelic spots come as a warning sign, and while the seizing does not necessarily hurt, the impact of it causes a slow, tedious, tiring recovery back to normal. My kind of normal.

It can take a while, sometimes weeks, for my vision and muscle memory to fully come back after a seizure. These are the times I rely on my family the most—for simply putting toothpaste on my toothbrush, or reading to me so I won't go mad sitting for hours in bed. I would not survive without my family, literally and figuratively. They wake me up for my morning medication and offer mental support, often laughing with me.

Truthfully, there are times when I feel like a burden or have moments of isolation knowing I can no longer do what I used to or what others can. Don't get me wrong, sometimes there is nothing I love more than to be alone to read a book. However, I have quite a lot of time to sit, think, and observe, including about how my younger sister has surpassed me in college and now has complete independence. It is bittersweet seeing my friends' graduation pictures. I feel a small pang in my heart at how my younger cousin is now taller than me and has taken my place in learning the cha-cha with my grandfather in our kitchen.

MELAS is classified as an "invisible disease" because I don't "look sick"—I don't have a bald head like many people with cancer do, use a wheelchair, or have another outwardly visible sign of illness. This leads people to assume I am lazy, anorexic, or that I could fix myself if I wanted to. I recently went to get my hair done and an older woman said, "Oh, so skinny," as she walked by me. I wanted to scream, "I am sick!" These assumptions are so frustrating and make me feel like I have no control over myself and the narrative others put on me. I could explain it in detail if they would take a second to stop and understand me—although that isn't something I should have to do either.

So, though it is hard sometimes, I remind myself to thrive in the little things. I appreciate every day. I know how fortunate I am to have family dinners, two silly dogs, nightly TV, and my own comfy bed. (Hospital beds certainly need reinvention!) When I can turn over in bed without a tube attached to me or take a shower without my mom holding me up, I am grateful. I love being able to read on my own, to explore and engage with the world through the pages of books even though I'm stuck in bed. And, most people don't truly understand the gift of being able to see! When the seizures steal my vision, sometimes for months at a time, my parents and grandparents read to me. I know and have seen people who are much worse off than I am, including others with mitochondrial diseases. But there are times when people ask me how I am doing, and I can only think, "Ask me tomorrow."

Still, the little things add up: watching my dogs play in the living room full of joy; eating grilled cheese and french fries in the car with my mom; my father helping me eat when I am blind, and the laughter we share when he misses my mouth. Little things are actually very big and meaningful.

I chose to write about this part of my life as a means of closure, or maybe as some form of inspiration. It is hard to inspire yourself to do something, never mind others, but hopefully this story can be a start for us both.

20

CRAWLING THROUGH THE CRUST

NIKKI BOND

AS THE BEEPING of the heart rate monitor slows like the drip-drip of molasses, my heart races in response. Murmurs from the doctors become clear in my ears.

"The baby's heart rate is dropping. We need to do a C-section."

"Get the O.R. ready," barks another doctor.

In the quickest slow-motion moment I've ever had, I am whisked away through swinging doors. Murmurs continue as I am wheeled into a large room with harsh lights. Doctors and nurses swarm around me—moving this and taking that. The green curtain appears before me. I can feel them touching my swollen belly.

Oh, my God—I can *feel* them. I cry out, "I feel you!"

More murmuring. "The epidural must be wearing off," one doctor mutters.

"We need to do this *now*," another urges.

The loudest voice in the room asserts, "Put her out!"

The glaring lights turn to gray matter when the mask is put on, like tying a warm scarf around my neck.

My mind drifts back to simpler days at Quentin Street, in Milton, Massachusetts—the place I spent every weekend, every school vacation, every summer, and any other time that my mother needed a break. I was there a lot. It was a place of safety, a place of love. The home of my two great aunts, Auntie Ma and Auntie Bea, sisters who never married. They love me. And I love them.

I'm waking up at Quentin Street. I'm eight years old, the sun splashing across my bed in the room I share with Auntie Bea. A big wooden rosary hangs on the wall above our beds. I look at the bureau across from the foot of our beds and see the familiar Saint Michael standing triumphantly with his sword drawn and his foot on the back of Satan's head. I inhale deeply and smell toast and maple syrup. I roll onto my side and heave myself out of bed.

The bathroom tile is pink and cold on my bare feet. The room smells strongly of Ivory soap and Yardley of London English Lavender.

I step down the stairs slowly, allowing my body to wake. I squint and rub my eyes as the smell of oatmeal with brown sugar and syrup fills my nose with pleasure.

Auntie Bea is at the stove, twirling a wooden spatula into a pan that's guilty of giving off the wafts of morning oatmeal. Auntie Ma is at the table with her cup of Pero, studying the morning news. She looks up over her paper and I take in her cat-green eyes and wrinkly face. She quickly winks at me and goes back to her paper.

Auntie Ma is old. She's in her eighties and I often worry how long I will have her. Her blocky, transparent hands are gnarled—fingers arthritic and riddled with spots. She wears gold-rimmed glasses that match her gold-dyed hair held upright by Aqua Net. She sits, relaxed, in an old house coat that is soft from thousands of washings.

I take my seat at the table and spread some ricotta on the toasted Scali bread. Auntie Bea plops a heaping spoonful of oatmeal into my bowl, and I grab the mason jar filled with milk, pouring a pool of it into the middle of my oatmeal. I take a big spoonful and delight in the juxtaposition of the cold milk separating from the hot oatmeal in my mouth.

Auntie Bea smiles at me and her right cheek gives way to a large dimple. Her eyes are large and bright blue below her eggshell eyelids. Her lips are full and wide, revealing a perfectly placed beauty mark above her lip.

"Good girl," she gleams.

She takes her seat and begins to eat the remaining oatmeal directly from the pot.

Auntie Ma's eyes dart toward her accusingly and she barks, "Bea! Don't be a jackass!"

Auntie Bea raising one pointed eyebrow in protest, says, "Mildred, I'm the one who washes the dishes. If I choose to eat from the pan, it's just that—my choice." And with that, she tilts her head back joyfully, closing her eyes, and scoops a large mound of oatmeal into her mouth.

Auntie Ma shakes her head in disapproval, and I just sit there eating, enjoying the moment and feeling loved.

Coming back to my body, my eyelids feel heavy; they resist commands to see my environment of cold, bare hospital room. To my right, I focus on my husband, Brian, holding our baby girl. He is crying, and my foggy brain notes that my daughter is limp in his arms. Maybe she's asleep.

Brian approaches the bed with Anya, and hands her carefully wrapped body to me. Words—"She didn't make it"—escape from his mouth as his tears fall onto Anya's swaddling blanket.

"She didn't make it," he repeats.

I hold my baby in my arms. I wrap and unwrap her. I scrutinize her entire perfect body—her perfect, reddish, curly hair. I hold her with a feral possessiveness as they come to take her away from me. I have to let them. I have to let her go. They take her to the place where babies that didn't make it go.

And just like that—she's gone.

Later, after I've been moved to a room, my doctor comes to visit me, explaining that I'm sick and they don't know why or what it is. They've taken blood and are awaiting lab results. The room fills with the stench of grief and confusion as a menagerie of nurses, doctors, and aides dance in and out. My room. It's on the maternity ward. I can hear them crying—the babies that made it. The babies that are alive.

My body is betraying me. I sink back into a place of unconsciousness, battling a sickness that no one yet understands.

I'm seventeen. My Auntie Ma has passed. Auntie Bea is still at 16 Quentin Street, and her mind has become increasingly more preoccupied with the past since she was diagnosed with dementia. I'm pregnant and I've dropped out of high school. Today's the day though. The day I drag my morning-sickness-riddled body to the community college to take my GED examination. Mother and I are speaking again and so she picks me up from my apartment and takes me to the college. My mother. We never really did get along. When I was born, she was homeless, and it was one of the many reasons my aunts took such a large role in raising me. Sometimes my mother and I hate each other like enemies entrenched in war, and other times we cling to each other because we're all we have.

I'm lying in the hospital bed, still not fully conscious, but I can hear the familiar voice of my obstetrician—she's on the phone.

"Brian? You need to come back to the hospital—she hasn't got much time—maybe an hour. We're losing her. I'm going back to the lab to await the results. Whatever this is, it's killing her."

I don't know how much time has passed when my obstetrician plows through the doors. She hops on my bed and examines my C-section incision where a red rash has been spreading for a couple of days. She yells to the nurse to give me morphine and immediately begins tearing my staples out one by one. "You have a serious staph infection, Nikki. We need to drain the wound."

Once the doctor finishes this attack on my wounds, she explains that they've discovered the exact bacteria that was growing exponentially throughout my body. The antibiotics they were giving me simply weren't strong enough to kill this super bug. It can be treated—but, because my body is weak, the treatment could kill me. It's a risk, but if they don't take it, I will die from the infection anyway.

I'm moved to another room on another floor, away from the babies and new moms. People in what look like hazmat suits come in and out of my new room. They poke and prod my body and take blood every few hours to see if the treatment is working.

Days go by and I grow stronger physically. I have little time to mourn my daughter as every bit of focus is simply on surviving—not for me, exactly, but for my sons at home. They're waiting for me. They need me.

I look out the window on my last day in the hospital and see a brilliant rainbow arching across the sky. It's in that very moment I just know I'll rise above this.

Over the next three years I develop a sense of who I am and where I want to be ... and then comes divorce. I leave my job as a restaurant manager and get a part-time job as an online banker so I can pursue full-time academics at my local community college. My three boys are a handful, but we have each other, and it works for us. Every Wednesday we go to dinner at our local Burger King. Embarrassingly, the staff gets to know us. I feel a sense of community.

One Wednesday, I'm in line with my three boys, waiting to order, when I glance up to the counter and notice a new manager standing there. My heart begins to hammer with excitement. A sense of familiarity seeps over my body like a warm blanket. Who is this strange, enigmatic creature standing before me?

I know, in this moment, that I have found my soulmate.

Russ picks me up for our first date on a warm October night. My house smells of freshly baked cookies. His presence in my home feels as natural as a best friend's. We drive to the beach where he encloses my hand in his. We walk, and laugh, and talk. In a fluid gesture, he cups my face in his hands and, like a thief, steals a kiss and my heart.

I surrender with euphoric abandon. I already know him—from a past life, a dream, or something else completely? I'm not sure. I just know that his hand touches my face and is like a balm on my wounds. Under the touch of his fingers, my worries melt away.

For the first time in my adult life, I do not feel like an expendable commodity.

We both have dreams that are left unfinished. He wants to be a teacher, and I want to be a social worker. We form a team and reach our goals together. Russ earns a Master's of Education, and I earn my Master's of Social Work. He loves my boys as his own, and we become the most beautiful blended family.

Best of all, he loves my Auntie Bea.

Auntie Bea. After all her years of raising me, she has come to the end of her life in our home. I awake one morning and hesitantly get out of bed, tiptoeing through the kitchen as though walking carefully will soften the impact of what I might find in the living room. Every time I checked on her through the night, her breathing had become more of a struggle.

Now, I stare at Auntie as she takes a breath. I count to sixteen, seventeen, eighteen, before she takes another breath. That's a long time in between. I feel for her heartbeat, and it is barely there. I try to take her pulse, but her veins are too constricted. She takes another breath. Twelve, thirteen, fourteen before her next.

I don't know how long I've been standing there. I don't know how many breaths I've counted—but, finally, my counting gets to thirty, thirty-one, thirty-two. I call Russ to my side. Maybe it was me. Maybe I wasn't watching right. *Auntie, breathe!* I stare at her for two minutes, until Russ puts his hands on my arms.

"Baby, she's gone," he says. I shake my head in disbelief—but she never takes another breath.

She was peaceful. She was content. She left this world to be with Jesus. It's all she ever wanted anyway.

I lie next to her for a long while. I ask her how she likes Anya. I ask her if heaven is beautiful. I keep her covered with several blankets. I kiss her cheek and stroke her silver hair and hear her responses clearly in my mind.

The hospice nurse arrives and pronounces her dead at 10:35 a.m., but I know she passed at 9:13 a.m. because I was counting. We clean her up a little and dress her in a pretty skirt, her blue blouse, and her blue sweater. Blue was her favorite color, the color of her eyes.

I will never get to see those glass-blue eyes again.

An hour later, the mortician comes to take her away. He scoops her up in his arms and puts her on the stretcher. They take her outside and ready her in the bag. I long to cover her up so she won't be cold, but he zips her up, and off she goes in the back of a black minivan. Off to the funeral home. In a bag.

Auntie Bea. The woman who slung me over her shoulder like a sack of potatoes and carried me home when I was four.

I was born into this world to a homeless mom and became a pregnant teenage dropout. I know what it's like to have only $13 for groceries, to be married to the wrong person, and to be living in opposition to my best path. I have withstood the loss of a child, and the pain of divorce. I watched my beloved aunties die before my eyes.

But I have loved, and been loved. I have been treasured, and cherished. I have risen when everything around me indicated I would fall. I have made myself more than anyone ever expected of me. I have crawled through the crust of life and reaped the delicious reward of happiness, success, and joy.

The journey isn't always easy. Sometimes, it feels easier to give in than to rise up. But the rise is always worth it, because even when our dear ones leave us, love remains.

21

INITIATION

KENDRA E. THORNBURY, MA

EVERY GIRL NEEDS an initiation to usher her across the threshold into adulthood, a marking of her entrance into becoming a woman.

Absent a deliberate pathway for such a passage, one is created by unseen forces. Often revealed through unwanted packages or even as a crisis, events are set in motion to force her into contending with a new self and a fresh set of responsibilities that accompany the transformed identity and heightened consciousness.

Whether she sees and accepts the confronting invitation is a choice that determines her destiny.

This was true for me. Thrust into a neurological "disorder," I was presented with an initiation I didn't even know I required.

I was twenty-two.

I'd recently traveled by car across the country from Minnesota to Washington state to finally discover what I was going to do with my life. The trouble was, I was confused and lost. Unbeknownst to me at the time, I had disowned my power and felt obliged to make decisions based on what I believed others wanted of me.

So, although I ventured thousands of miles to start a new life, I still lived in the body and consciousness I so badly ached to leave behind. I was grossly disconnected from myself, and I didn't know how to identify or trust my own sense of knowing or direction.

My studies at my new college in women's spirituality, experiential education, and organizational development gave me glimmers of optimism, sparking a belief in the potential that I could actually design a future born of genuine passion and meaning. But, I had enormous obstacles to overcome.

I desired to break out, so I sought relief in self-medication—successfully remaining sedated by a world hell-bent on keeping me a stranger to myself.

Alcohol was my balm. When I drank, the out-of-control feeling I experienced *felt* like freedom. I didn't realize it was an undeveloped type of freedom, reckless and without roots to keep me tethered. I was convinced the careless risks were worth it.

For those few years out of high school, drinking was the only time I could soften the torment of being human, soothe my harsh mind, and liberate my free spirit.

My body was not my home. I did not belong to myself. I was a wild one stuck in a fabricated world, and I believed the confinements and restrictions were outcomes of my own inadequacies, my own imperfections. I lived in the frenzied haze of dissociation, the secret shame of disembodiment, and the restless angst of disconnection. I had a relentless urgency to get free.

I was nowhere near what my heart and Soul wanted, and I was terrified I'd never find what that was. I craved it, and I grappled for it, but I was equally obsessed with finding relief.

I did eventually return to myself.

It started with a seizure that shook me to my core.

A thrashing wake-up. A wave of convulsions. A totally out-of-control explosion.

I didn't know it at the time, but the me who was bound and chained craved to be wild and free, and she had to bust the fuck out. She'd reached the tipping point. I'd become an inhospitable environment to myself.

Life was seizing me. Taking me back into the land of the living. Reclaiming possession of me. The convulsions were like a shaman's rattle, shaking me, and without recollection of these spaces in time, I was lost to a wild moment of escape.

Then I had another seizure. And another. And another.

When I met with my first neurologist after a series of tests, he told me I had epilepsy, wrote a prescription ... and that was it. No holistic approach, just a pharmaceutical one.

Rather than shrink from the diagnosis and give my authority over to the experts—who had given me no guidance on how to thrive as I moved forward, only a piece of paper with a prescription—something in me woke up.

So, I fired that neurologist. And I fired the tyrannical voices in my head that dismissed my inner knowing.

The Universe was literally shaking me, "Wake up!" I had a choice, so I chose aliveness. I realized I could take charge of my health, and by doing so, I could take charge of my life.

My commitment? To live as fully as possible by devouring information and experiences to transcend limitations associated with the label "illness," and to use my diagnosis as a wake-up call and a favorable opening.

Initially, I was faced with the looming feeling that I was destined for a long life of limits. The constraint I felt when met with prescriptions, people imposing opinions about what I couldn't do anymore, and the narrow view of the kind of life before me was suffocating and oppressive.

The cautionary tales taunted me.

I didn't want my main identity to be "Epileptic." I didn't want to be dependent on doctors or external authorities. I didn't want to be placed into an even more confined box of existence. I didn't want to be told what was or wasn't possible, given this label. I didn't want to be medicated for the rest of my life.

I didn't want to settle for a "just enough" reality.

Even more importantly, I was scared I'd increasingly become a shell of a being, cautiously tiptoeing through existence and popping pills in a constant effort to avoid seizures.

I was already lost, insecure, and using tactics like drinking excessive amounts of alcohol to relax and numb out. Most of the time, I was fearful and vigilantly trying to figure out how to play the game so I would belong and feel safe. To feel safe, I gave my authority to others.

Clearly, this was a reckoning. An ordeal designed by my Soul to come to terms with myself.

My orientation could not be, "I am an epileptic." I desired to understand how to build a thriving, healthy life.

I had an inner sense, a gut feeling that there just *had* to be another way. If I didn't get to the root of it and truly heal the imbalance my body was pointing to, the symptoms and suffering would only intensify. Instead of questing to get rid of the problem, I embarked on a journey of self-discovery and awakening. I stopped fighting my body and started working in cooperation with it.

I used the seizures as a doorway to transformation, unlocking the key to my well-being. I knew it was my responsibility to create the environment within to nurture the conditions for my health—in all respects. Nothing external was going to provide this. It was time to stop deceiving myself and own my personal agency.

With *no* satisfaction in the prescribed life being handed to me, a burning holy desire was ignited. I became a proactive, conscious creator. I faced the challenges, embraced the wake-up call, got real with myself, stopped bad habits, and upped my self-care, big time.

An intelligence began to reveal itself, a deeper knowing inside I started listening to and trusting.

The seizures brought extreme migraines, and sometimes, after a seizure in the night, I'd wake up and my tongue would be cut and bloody from the convulsions.

I knew I needed a holistic strategy and body work to heal and form new neural patterns, so I sought a woman neurologist with an integrative patient-centered approach, and started to see a chiropractor. These resources changed the course of my life forever. I was supported in sincere outcomes for lasting health. I actively formed new wiring and harmonious circuitry, aligning my nervous system with its optimal state.

I became more selective with my time, with what and who I exposed myself to. No more alcohol or substances for me. Healing required that I no longer numbed my feelings.

Soulful poems like "The Journey" by Mary Oliver offered sweet chants of encouragement: "One day, you finally knew what you had to do." That day had arrived for me. The books I was studying opened my mind and helped me recognize that, on some level, being diagnosed with epilepsy was a blessing.

Seizures were a doorway into a new reality.

Gradually, I built my own formula for health. I studied nutrition and learned how food is medicine. I eliminated foods not optimal for my system and stopped eating processed foods, dairy, gluten, and sugar. I stopped drinking alcohol completely.

I didn't feel deprived. Instead, I felt empowered and renewed.

The change didn't end with my nourishment, though. I reinvented my mindset. I did intensive cleanses. I took up yoga. I communed with nature. I deepened my spiritual path.

I read material that exposed me to the inherent ability of my body to heal, whole systems design, natural and Universal law, the Divine Feminine, and the interconnectedness of life, which expanded my paradigm so greatly that there was no turning back.

Rather than fleeing from the dis-ease and feelings that led to my misalignment, I leaned into the rich possibilities that allowed true health to emerge. I realized I had a built-in capacity to repair and recover. That I had the power to completely reverse my symptoms and flourish.

The veil lifted, I accessed my primal innate intelligence and became loyal to the integrity of my being.

I came to know and trust my body's wisdom as a reliable Source of information and guidance. I discovered how to use the realm of my Soul and the subtleties of my feelings and sensations to make choices of the highest value to my essential and most authentic self.

As I created my new life, I did take medication for about a year, even though I didn't like how it made me feel. Medication had its place—but this journey was about me becoming a conscious creator of my own reality and learning how to influence and shape that reality. Medication was a bridge, not a bypass or a solution. It helped settle the symptoms just enough so I could do the work my body was inviting me to do.

I didn't passively sit back feeling sorry for myself. I didn't resign to the belief that something was wrong. I didn't allow victim consciousness to reduce me to a helpless state anymore.

My wise self knew the truth. This was an auspicious opportunity, and I was going to deliberately determine the health, the life, and the future I wanted!

This was the initiation into my ripening maturation, into active creation. It would take years to truly become freer and more sovereign in all areas of my life, but this defining moment was where it all began.

Today, I look back on that fateful time in wonder and gratitude.

On some level, it seems incomprehensible that at such a young age and stage of life, I could heal myself and reclaim my personal agency. Yet I understand now that the capacity and strength I summoned are natural to initiation.

I put an end to underestimating myself, intentionally went beyond the illusion of fear, paid attention to the sacred message, and alchemized my wounds into wisdom.

I took 100 percent responsibility for my reality, and my brazen rebel finally got to channel her unapologetic fire into a worthwhile pursuit, growing into her iconic wildness for the greater good. She defied convention, blazing a trail that suited her unique design.

Looking back, I can see how my desperation for release gave rise to an explosion of energy. It surged through me. The chaos and eventual unraveling gave way to new meaning.

Looking back, I can see the young woman straddling the conflicting desires of control and wildness. A girl struggling without guidance or a deliberate passage into the realm of womanhood. She longed to be unencumbered and unfettered by rules, yet was bound by the unconscious agreement to give herself up and conceal her greatness in service to false security.

And when the Universe shook her—literally—she finally answered, and that was the beginning of a new life for her, for me. It was a catalyst, the initiation required to remember, honor, actualize, and prosper from who she truly is. I could finally rest in my skin. I've been naturally seizure-free for thirty years and actively creating since that Divine moment.

EDITOR'S NOTE

BRYNA HAYNES

I STOOD IN FRONT of a room full of yoga students, trembling and utterly terrified.

Luckily, none of them could see me; they were resting in śavāsana, eyes closed, breathing peacefully after our heated vinyasa class. None of them had any idea what I was about to do.

Although I'd been teaching yoga asana classes for nearly a year at that point, I had only recently discovered the practice of bhakti yoga, the yoga of devotion. Included in that practice is kirtan, the chanting or singing of divine mantras. I immediately fell in love. These mantras spoke to my soul.

And today, for the first time, I was about to share one of these mantras with my students.

As a lifelong musician, performing was nothing new for me.

Growing up, I played in various bands and orchestras. When I was thirteen, I picked up my dad's old Gibson and started teaching myself the guitar. Several years of open mics, busking in coffee shops, and the occasional real gig followed.

And then, I met a boy. He was a musician, too—a drummer in a somewhat successful band, and a wannabe lead singer. For reasons I may never know or understand, he didn't like it when I played.

"No one wants to hear *you*," he'd sneer when I broke out my guitar at a party.

"Can't you write something less ... depressing?" he'd ask when I tentatively shared a new original song.

Being eighteen to his twenty-five, and more than a little socially awkward, I listened. Of course he would know better than I did what people liked and wanted to hear.

And I wanted *so badly* to be heard.

I started singing less and less. Even after I broke up with that boyfriend, I still couldn't convince myself that anyone would care about my music. "No one wants to hear you" became my story—the story I told myself whenever the subject of music came up.

In my next relationship—also with a musician—the dynamic was different: he encouraged me, but also openly admitted he was jealous of my talent. Because I was young and in love, I decided that the solution to this issue was to make him comfortable, and to confine my musical expression to the spare bedroom of our crappy apartment. After all, that approach fit comfortably with the story I already carried.

That small room quickly filled with instruments: a digital piano, multiple guitars, a flute, an electric violin. None of them ever saw the bright lights of a stage. If our neighbors heard me playing my heart out when my significant other was at work, they never said so.

It was easy to sing, play, and compose in secret. Alone, I could bare my soul without risk. What no one could hear, no one could criticize.

Years went by. That boyfriend and I got married, and I soon discovered the dark secrets of his trauma and addictions. Putting out fires—figuratively, and sometimes literally—in our home became a full-time job. I was constantly on high alert, walking on eggshells, dodging fists and words that cut like knives, trying to understand how my once-promising life could have become so bleak. I stopped composing. I stopped playing. It was all I could do to keep up with my multiple jobs—which, by that time, included teaching yoga—and still put on a bright face so my friends and loved ones wouldn't see how bad things were.

And then, I found kirtan.

It was easier to sing the mantras than it had been to sing my own songs. These weren't *my* words, but recitations of the many names of God. They couldn't be dismissed or belittled; there was no way for them to be "not good enough." They were armor for my broken heart. And yet, when I sang these mantras, I felt my soul open in the same ways it used to do, back when I was a poet and all the world was inspiration.

Om Namo Bhagavate Vāsudevāya. Praise to the indwelling one—the one who is becoming enlightened.

At first, I sang the mantras in the car. Then, in the shower. I sang along with my favorite kirtan artists, and began composing melodies of my own. I ordered a harmonium from India and learned to play it.

Then, the owner of the yoga studio where I worked caught me singing while I cleaned up after class.

"You need to share this," she said. (Thank you, Christine.)

Which is how I found myself standing in front of forty of my beloved yoga students, shaking like a leaf, unable to open my mouth and yet knowing that, if I didn't, I would be condemning myself to another year, another decade—maybe even a lifetime—of silence.

That day, I found my voice again.

It seemed like such a small thing, to open my mouth and let sound come out. But I can say with certainty that it was one of the scariest, and bravest, things I've ever done.

I faced my fear, and won.

Half the class didn't even realize it was me singing; they thought I was playing something on my iPod. The other half were encouraging and gracious about my offering. And then, once everyone else had gone, my dear friend and fellow yoga teacher hugged me and wept, because she said my voice felt like love.

In that moment, I knew that I could never stay silent again, no matter how afraid I might be.

That day, I began to reclaim my voice. Not only in a musical sense, but across my whole life. Within a year, my marriage was over; it couldn't survive me standing in my truth. Some friendships changed, and others ended. I started wondering what it would be like to tell a new story—a story of worthiness, of confidence, of a woman whose voice could inspire change in others.

That was fourteen years ago—and a lifetime ago.

Today, I have the privilege of supporting thought leaders from all over the globe to reclaim their voices and tell their own transformational stories through the medium of world-changing books. I just celebrated ten years of marriage to my husband Matthew, who not only cherishes my voice but fully believes in my every dream and crazy scheme. Together, we have two outspoken, articulate daughters whom, I'm certain, will someday run the world. And, I'm happy to say, I still lead the occasional kirtan session.

When we change the stories we tell ourselves, *everything* changes.

The women whose stories you have just read have been through their own trials and triumphs. They have been silenced, as I was. They have been hurt. And yet, they prevailed. They learned to *rise*.

The "rise" doesn't start on the outside. It's a decision, made from a place deep within our souls, to be and express the most vibrant, complete, and dynamic version of ourselves. Even when it's hard. Even when others don't understand. Even when we are shaking too hard to hold the microphone.

This is how HERstory is created: through the willingness of brave women to share their stories, even when we aren't yet certain of the ending. By authentically sharing our inner worlds, we show others that they are not alone, and that no matter how dark things may seem, there is always a way to rise.

May this book inspire you to share your own story, Reader, because your story matters. Your voice matters. *You* matter.

And HERstory is waiting to be made.

With love,
Bryna Haynes
Chief Editor, CEO, and founder, WorldChangers Media Inc.

ABOUT KIM FULLER
& BORN TO RISE

KIM FULLER is a mindful photographer, mindfulness and story coach, author, TEDx speaker, and the founder of Born to Rise™. Her passion is to help women stand in their power, their story, and their beauty so they can live a confident and peaceful life. She uses photography to mirror the beauty she sees in each woman, empowering them to show up authentically in business and life.

Kim gives women a platform to share their personal stories with a live audience so they can process, release, and transform from victim to hero. She provides mindful tools through her Art of the P.A.U.S.E. Method that invite women to slow down and look carefully inward. This enables them to expand in creativity, intuition, peace, and joy, and release their fears, judgments, and assumptions of themselves and others.

Kim leads workshops and story exchanges in the DEI space, with women's groups and at conferences. She has been a keynote speaker and workshop facilitator for Chubb insurance, Bank Newport, Bryant Women's Summit, the United Way, IGT, Adidas, Day One, and many other organizations. She has been a guest on several podcasts, radio shows, and television spots speaking about mindfulness and the power of storytelling.

One of Kim's greatest gifts is that she's a great hugger. She is a mother of three children, one of whom is adopted and is her greatest spiritual teacher. Her first book, *Finding,* tells the story of her journey with this young boy and the Dalai Lama.

BORN TO RISE is Kim's passion. She believes if we can see the greatest qualities in ourselves by unraveling unhelpful stories, assumptions, and judgments, we can heal and rise to our greatest potential. When we are healed, we lead our lives with more love, compassion, and empathy. When we share our stories we connect more deeply, educate others, and bridge the divides that keep us from understanding those who seem different than ourselves.

Kim also feels the voices of women need to be amplified to balance the stories that have been told for centuries by men. Women's stories tend to explore themes such as community, collaboration, and compassion whereas many of our historical stories were about wars, power, and control. We need both versions of life to understand the best possibility for all people and the planet.

Discover Born to Rise's mission and live storytelling events at www.borntorise.live.

ABOUT THE
AUTHORS

(IN ORDER OF APPEARANCE)

ALEXA GORMAN has been writing, reading, creating, organizing, and chasing dogs in Connecticut for most of her life. A graduate of Stony Brook University's School of Journalism, she quickly learned the hard-hitting life of a reporter was not for her. She's spent the last nine years as a saleswoman, social media marketer, content creator, energy healer, and virtual assistant, before combining her skills to provide strategic launch and marketing support for creative businesses, including WorldChangers Media. Read more of Alexa's thoughts on Instagram @by_alexagorman or on Substack at alexagorman.substack.com.

PARCHELLE TASHI is an accomplished and award-winning video producer who started her career as a high school math teacher before venturing into video production over a decade ago. Based in San Diego, she founded The Author's Leverage, a team of experienced professionals in learning design, high-quality video production, and learning management systems who support authors in turning their bestselling books into premium online courses. When not producing, Parchelle enjoys playing pickleball, cooking, tutoring math, attending live music events, and traveling. Her mission is to create impactful learning experiences that inspire positive change. Learn more at www.theauthorsleverage.com.

MICHELLE LEMOI is a strategic catalyst, visionary leader, speaker, author, corporate trainer and consultant, and entrepreneur with over thirty years' experience in the construction industry, including leading her own company, Lemoi Erectors, Inc., from 2009 to 2016. Today, she is CEO and Founder of Elevate Women In Construction, which provides training, resources, and support for women in male-dominated industries who want to move from surviving to thriving in their environments. Michelle provides corporate training and consulting, and is a sought-after speaker. She has authored two contributory chapters in bestselling anthologies, and is currently working on her solo book. Learn more at www.elevatewic.com.

JEANNIE SPIRO is a business coach, speaker, and host of *The Midlife CEO Podcast*. She specializes in teaching women how to take the complication out of creating recurring revenue and break six and seven figures in their coaching business. As a former sales executive, Jeannie combined her sales and speaking experience gained from supporting thousands of clients in her twenty-five-year career and developed speaking and sales focused coaching programs to help women simplify the path to more revenue in their business. Dedicated to aging positively, Jeannie lives with her family on the Rhode Island coastline. Learn more at www.JeannieSpiro.com.

RENÉE POIRIER is a self-discovering twenty-five-year-old drawn to the ability of sport to build confidence in young women. Renée is a 2019 graduate of the United States Military Academy at West Point, where she was a two-year softball team captain. While stationed at Fort Bliss, TX, Renee also coached for the Desert Gators, a highly competitive youth softball program. After serving her Army obligation, she jumped headfirst into her continued passion for the mentorship of young athletes in a sports-driven career. She is currently earning a Master's degree in Sports Industry Management from Georgetown University, and offers private softball instruction at Planet Fastpitch, LLC.

DOMINEY DREW is a spiritual advisor, author, speaker and intuitive healer. High performers in every industry hire her to break down the current paradigms in their inner world which keep them from real fulfillment and maximum impact. Dominey is the premier in rapid results coaching; her direct, intuitive approach is unlike anything else in the industry. Through a process of profound self-discovery, she solves in mere minutes issues that have carried on for decades. She's been featured in *Forbes* and *Entrepreneur* for her work, and now travels the world teaching those who seek massive transformation. Connect with Dominey at www.domineydrew.com.

KIM HAYES is a creative and results-oriented problem solver who is praised for her ability to develop visionary solutions to complex business and technology challenges. She was featured in the December 2021 issue of *Rhode Island Monthly* as a recipient of the Tech10 Award for Innovation in Technology. You can find Kim speaking at various forums, mentoring emerging leaders, volunteering at Diversity, Equity and Inclusion (DEI) events and spending quality time with her family. Kim is a loving mom to two amazing daughters, Ashley and Juliana. She lives in Cranston, Rhode Island with her wife, Michelle, daughter Juliana, and their miniature goldendoodle, Princess. Find her on LinkedIn @khayes629.

JULIANA HAYES never thought she'd be a published author at sixteen years old. Currently an accomplished high school scholar and National Honor Society member, an avid sports player, and a member of numerous academic clubs, Juliana's passion for the arts has expressed itself through music and literature from an early age. Whether writing poetry or song, participating in book club and chorus club, pestering her favorite English teacher, or indulging her love of acting through her favorite school activity, Mock Trial, Juliana's love for the arts informs her life. She has also had the opportunity to produce her music on numerous occasions. Overall, Juliana considers herself a well-rounded and passionate individual ready to explore all facets that life presents her.

JESS SPINO is a Fractional CMO/COO and systems and branding expert with a diverse background in traditional and digital marketing and media. Over the past six years, she's supported some of the biggest names in the online space in scaling to seven figures and beyond. Her strengths include personal and business branding, funnel building and optimization, design, content creation, social media management, organic marketing, and sales. With a B.S. in Communications Planning and Evaluation from Cornell University and an EdM from SUNY at Buffalo, Jess's approach is equally creative and strategic. She's passionate about building systems that create maximum efficiency and allow entrepreneurs to spend more time in their zone of genius. She lives in western New York with her husband, two daughters, and her lovable mutt. For more information, visit www.jessspino.com.

CHRISTINE AMERMAN is passionate about helping impact-driven entrepreneurs attract their next clients by being value-driven podcast guests. She and her clients have generated over $1 million as podcast guests, and she's has been recognized as the best in the world at podcast guesting by seven-figure founders like John Lee Dumas, Dana Wilde, and Andrew Kroeze. A media expert for over two decades, she's helped broadcast the Olympic Games, produced an award-winning documentary for PBS, and has been featured in *Inc., Business Insider, Bustle, The Huffington Post* and on over 100 podcasts, in addition to hosting her own top-rated show, *No One's Ever Asked Me That*. Connect with Christine at www.lifewithpassion.com.

JENN EDDEN, CHHC is a certified holistic health coach of twenty years, sugar addiction expert, founder of The Sugar Freedom Method®, and author of *Woman Unleashed*. Jenn's zone of genius is teaching forty- to sixty-year-old busy female professionals how to live their best life by reducing inflammation, managing sugar addiction, and shedding stubborn weight for good using her five-step trademarked process, The Sugar Freedom Method—all without deprivation, denial or dieting. Learn more about how you can look and feel your best self again at www.jecoaching.com.

DIANE CAINE is first a wife, momma, and mammie. Professionally, she brings two decades of global leadership experience working for Fortune 100 companies. Diane is a highly sought-after speaker and values-driven facilitator, recently joining the Half Full, LLC team where she helps teams and individuals overcome obstacles through team building, culture building and retreat planning. Diane holds a B.S. in Business Management from Johnson & Wales University, and is certified in the Maxwell Method of Leadership coaching, DISC Human Behavior, and Six Sigma Green Belt. She is a contributing author in the recent book, *Shining a Light on Grief*. Diane lives in Rhode Island with her husband Bobby; they are the proud parents of four children and two grandsons. Follow her on LinkedIn @dianemcaine.

ASHLEY COOK is a professional storyteller, copywriter, and copy mentor with over fifteen years of sales and marketing experience. She's crafted sales material for Fortune 500 companies and coached six- and seven-figure entrepreneurs on how to communicate their value to their clients. As a seminary graduate and avid writer, Ashley believes in the power of words. She now helps women who have been hurt by religion to tell their story so they can feel supported, have peace with their beliefs, and remember they're not alone. Learn more about Ashley at www.ashleycook.co.

LISA ROCHE is a Spiritual Consultant specializing in Channeled Healing, helping clients who are ready to experience profound change in their lives. Lisa is a skilled Oracle who delivers higher guidance to help you get to the next level of your existence so you can live a life of purpose. She works with a select number of people who are ready to accept the advice given to them by their spiritual guides, and who are ready to show up in their lives empowered and in their highest expression. Lisa is also the cofounder of Spirit Calling, an online community based platform that provides support, guidance, and education for individuals navigating through their awakening journey. Find Lisa and her programs at www.LisaGRoche.com and www.Spirit-Calling.com.

PORTIA MICHELE is a Peak Performance coach, podcast host, a speaker, and energetic practitioner who empowers impact-driven leaders to unlock their essence and find more joy, ease and peace in the way they run their businesses. It is often said that leadership style, career path, and overall well-being can be amplified and success accelerated through constant and loving constructive feedback—and that's where a good coach like Portia kicks in. With her ten-plus years of experience supporting hundreds of impact driven CEOs, she provides support in planning, self-discovery, operational integration, executive function, and increased productivity tactics that enable them to overcome negative emotions, harness their gifts, and maximize their impact. Learn more on Instagram @portia.thecreator.

LINDA LINDQUIST is a world-champion sailor, strategist, speaker, bridge-builder, professional EOS® implementer, philosopher, and mentor. She blazed trails in the all-male world of yacht racing, making history as a member of America3, the first and only all-women's team to compete for the America's Cup. As the founder of Courageous Thinking Inc., Linda guides individuals and organizations to successfully navigate change and build thriving growth-oriented companies. She teaches that a life of inquiry is the access to our possibility and joy; she is ferociously committed to helping people find their purpose and greatness, and to live their biggest lives. Linda is also a life-long humanitarian activist; most recently she provided support to Ukrainian refugees in Eastern Europe. Learn more about Linda at www.cgthink.com.

KELLY WEST is a senior systems analyst in the Information Systems department for Beacon Mutual Insurance. She's also a certified fitness instructor and yoga teacher, a Reiki I and II certified practitioner, and a student of Transcendental Meditation. After losing her mother in 2015, followed by the loss of her husband just three weeks later, she found herself faced with an unbelievable amount of grief. Going within helped her heal her pain and rebuild her life. Now, she loves to help others discover their own inner healing paths through yoga. In her spare time, Kelly loves travel and exploration, going to live concerts, giving back to her community by serving on the board of Amenity Aid, and hanging out with her two fur babies, Sylvester and Winnie. Follow Kelly on Facebook @kelly.barrette.5

CHRISTINE GALLO is a joy-filled, mindful mom who lives in Northern RI with her husband Dan and two wonderful sons, Ever and Jasper. She was a public school educator for seventeen years before leaving the classroom to focus on her family and mental health. Today, Christine is a trauma-sensitive yoga and mindfulness facilitator for children and adults, and leads international yoga retreats with her sister, Cathleen. You can find her on Instagram @sunflowersoulsyoga and her blog at www.SunflowersandSynchronicity.wordpress.com.

FELICIA MESSINA-D'HAITI is a Feng Shui and Soul Coach/Teacher, speaker, award-winning educator and contributing author of several best-selling books. Denise Linn, award-winning author of *Sacred Space,* says, "Felicia is a remarkable teacher and practitioner! She knows how to get to the core of an issue quickly and easily; her ability to implement transformations in the lives of others is inspiring. I'm continually in awe of the abilities of this compassionate woman!" Using knowledge gained from more than twenty certifications with her own journeys of discovery, Felicia supports people in clearing the physical, mental, emotional, and spiritual blockages from their lives. Learn more at www.feliciadhaiti.com.

MARY JANE MILICI is a vibrant twenty-three-year old who grew up in Portsmouth, RI. After a childhood filled with school, modeling, painting, and performing classical ballet with the Newport Academy of Dance and the Island Moving Company, she was diagnosed in 2019 with MELAS disease following a massive stroke which temporarily took her vision and mobility. During her recovery, her grandmother brought paints and canvases to the house, and MJ began to paint; this helped build her strength and gave her a new vision. With the help of her family, she founded a greeting card company, Happy Little Card Store, the proceeds of which support the United Mitochondrial Disease Foundation (UMDF) and others struggling with mitochondrial diseases. Visit www.HappyLittleCardStore. com to learn more.

NIKKI BOND is a licensed clinical social worker in Rhode Island, as well as a therapist, energy healer, content creator, health and wellness expert, and life coach. Helping people overcome anxiety, depression, panic, and OCD is her passion. Nikki uses a combination of evidence-based therapeutic interventions, energy work, and life experience to help people live their best life and live confidently in their bodies. When not serving others, Nikki enjoys walking, listening to books, and spending time with her large family.

KENDRA THORNBURY, MA is an international highly-acclaimed coach, spiritual guide, speaker, facilitator, humanitarian, and entrepreneur blazing a wealth revolution. She helps Soul-centered, high achieving women and legacy leaders create spiritual and financial freedom while being true to who they are. Deeply devoted to Feminine reclamation as an integral force of change and evolution, her unconventional approaches lead women to build six- and seven-figure businesses grounded in timeless wisdom, purposeful contribution, and personal liberation. She facilitates sacred experiences that awaken women's natural power and sovereignty, including co-leading "The River," a deep wilderness adventure passed on by her mentor. Learn more about Kendra's work at www.kendrathornbury.com.

ABOUT THE PUBLISHER

FOUNDED IN 2021 by Bryna Haynes, WorldChangers Media is a boutique publishing company focused on "Ideas for Impact." We know that great books change lives, topple outdated paradigms, and build movements. Our commitment is to deliver superior-quality transformational nonfiction by, and for, the next generation of thought leaders.

Ready to write and publish your thought leadership book with us? Learn more at www.WorldChangers.Media.

CPSIA information can be obtained
at www.ICGtesting.com
Printed in the USA
BVHW030000250423
662941BV00001B/1

9 781955 811392